Your Teacher Leadership Journey

Build your success as a teacher leader with the practical advice in this book. Award-winning educator Melissa Collins shows how you can grow in your role by fostering relationships with colleagues, organizations, and mentors. She also spotlights rock star educators. She offers thorough advice on a wide variety of topics such as finding the right support, building your reputation, reinventing yourself, knowing your purpose, and developing leadership mindsets. She also explains how to manage your time wisely, build a network, enact purposeful practice, and, most of all, dare to dream. Appropriate for teachers at any level of their career who want to take on a larger role in their school or beyond as well as for administrators, district leaders, and teacher organizations to learn how to support or develop teacher leaders. The book's honest anecdotes and step-by-step suggestions will put teacher leaders on the right path, so that teacher leaders can develop in their careers and help their students thrive.

Melissa Collins is an elementary school teacher in Memphis, TN, where she is constantly amazed by her students' curiosity about the world around them. Melissa has been the recipient of several awards and honors, including Amazon Future Engineer Teacher of the Year, National University Award, Harriet Sanford Award, National Board Fellowship Program, the Global Teacher Prize Finalist (Top 50), the Presidential Award for Excellence in Science Teaching, the National Science Teaching Association (NSTA) Sylvia Shugrue Award, and the NSTA-Shell Urban Development Award. She was inducted into the National Teacher Hall of Fame in 2020.

T0386498

Your Teacher Leadership Journey

A Blueprint for Growth and Success

Melissa Collins

Routledge
Taylor & Francis Group

NEW YORK AND LONDON

Cover image: © Getty Images

First published 2023
by Routledge
605 Third Avenue, New York, NY 10158

and by Routledge
4 Park Square, Milton Park, Abingdon, Oxon, OX14 4RN

Routledge is an imprint of the Taylor & Francis Group, an informa business

© 2023 Melissa Collins

The right of Melissa Collins to be identified as author of this work has been asserted in accordance with sections 77 and 78 of the Copyright, Designs and Patents Act 1988.

All rights reserved. No part of this book may be reprinted or reproduced or utilised in any form or by any electronic, mechanical, or other means, now known or hereafter invented, including photocopying and recording, or in any information storage or retrieval system, without permission in writing from the publishers.

Trademark notice: Product or corporate names may be trademarks or registered trademarks, and are used only for identification and explanation without intent to infringe.

Library of Congress Cataloging-in-Publication Data
Names: Collins, Melissa (Elementary school teacher), author.
Title: Your teacher leadership journey : a blueprint for growth and success / Melissa Collins.
Description: New York, NY : Routledge, 2022. | Identifiers: LCCN 2022000832 (print) | LCCN 2022000833 (ebook) | ISBN 9781032134963 (hardback) | ISBN 9781032117355 (paperback) | ISBN 9781003229537 (ebook)
Subjects: LCSH: Educational leadership. | Teachers--Professional relationships. | Teaching--Vocational guidance.
Classification: LCC LB2806 .C535 2022 (print) | LCC LB2806 (ebook) | DDC 371.2/011--dc23/eng/20220310
LC record available at https://lccn.loc.gov/2022000832
LC ebook record available at https://lccn.loc.gov/2022000833

ISBN: 978-1-032-13496-3 (hbk)
ISBN: 978-1-032-11735-5 (pbk)
ISBN: 978-1-003-22953-7 (ebk)

DOI: 10.4324/9781003229537

Typeset in Palatino
by KnowledgeWorks Global Ltd.

Dedication

To my son, Devon. I love you forever! You are and will always be my baby!

To my mom (rest in love) and dad, Patricia and Stanley Collins. You have been inspirational to my teacher leadership journey.

To my sisters, Pam and Jennifer. You are both beautiful inside and out!

Contents

Acknowledgments

On my road to teacher leadership, it took a collective effort from family, friends, my school community, district, state department of education, and educational organizations to guide me on my journey. They provided me with a tremendous amount of support, encouragement, and guidance.

Teachers around the world, you are special, and I am so excited that we are working together to change the world. I appreciate each of you!

The team at Routledge and Lauren Davis, I am so thankful that you gave me the opportunity to share my story and the stories of several teacher leaders. You truly believe in building the capacity of teacher leaders.

Mom (Patricia Collins-rest in love), you are my hero! You showed me how to walk in faith while looking for a brighter day. Your strength and courage were contagious! I love you so much and I will live forever by your affirmation "keep it moving." Dad (Stanley Collins), thank you so much for pushing me to strive for greatness. You have both been my biggest cheerleaders! I am very grateful for your love and support.

My son (Devon Robinson), I truly love you! I have enjoyed watching you develop into an amazing human being. I soar to new heights because of you. Keep showing the world your unique talents. Devon's sister, Kathryn Campbell (my bonus daughter), I am so proud of all your accomplishments.

My sisters (Jennifer and Pam Collins), you are both so encouraging. Whenever I need you, you are always there for me. Thanks for your continuous support and love!

My Godchildren (Destinee Delaney, Colton Benjamin Stephens, Isabella Chrisette Stephens, and LeNorah Antoinette Stephens). I love you very much!

My sister-friends (Dr. Doretha Piper Allen, Shannon Allen, Chelsea Brown, Monica Brown, Ariel Nevilles-Gray, Latosha Guy,

Tanya Hill, Franchesca King [fly high, butterfly], Carmelita King, Anntriniece Napper, Sonya Cleaves-Newsom, Destine Peoples, Andrea Shannon, Erica Stephens, Adrianne Sublett, Lavette Ward, Melanie James, Jasmine Williams-Holston, and my beloved sister-circle), you have been so supportive throughout my teaching career. Your words of encouragement keep me focused on my teacher leadership journey.

My mentors (Shirley Echols and Frances Jones), you have been the wind beneath my wings. Shirley Echols, you were my first mentor, and you helped me to survive my first years of teaching. You were my perfect match, and you continue to support me throughout my teaching career. Frances Jones, you have prayed with and for me. You have helped me through many momentous occasions. Whenever I need you, you are always there for me. I am so grateful for your love and strength.

To my maternal grandparents (Earlene [my guardian angel] and Timothy Ham), you both inspired me to become whatever I wanted to be. You both gave me encouraging words to always move forward in life. I love you both dearly. Thanks to my paternal grandparents (Sarah [rest in love] and Samuel Thomas Collins [rest in peace]) for encouraging me to continue my education. I love you both!

To my Aunts and Uncles Debra (Steve) Dukes, Tonya (Tony) Lovett, Barbara and Willie Williams (rest in love), Pat (Michael) Jordan, and Tina Collins, and Timothy Ham, Alfonza (rest in love) Ham, James (Sharon) Ham, Eric (Allegra) Ham, Derick (Keisha) Ham, Dennis Ham (rest in love) (Nancy), Alfred Collins, Gerald (Gloria) Collins, Christopher Collins (rest in love), thank you for your guidance and support over the years. Thanks to all my family and friends who continue to inspire me to dream big!

To Barbara King, Gwen Price, and Toni Stephens, I love you all for being three of the best Godmothers ever! Your words of encouragement give me strength.

Dr. Nico West, thanks for being my STEM mentor and aiding our STEM students at my school. When I need you, you are always available to lend your time.

Thanks, Laura Bradley, Heather Bryson, Harriet Sanford, Katherine Basset, Amanda Upton, Sara Sneed and Peggy Brookins, for always supporting and celebrating with me.

To the many organizations who supported my career and allowed me to serve in leadership roles, I thank you for believing in me!

My first school principal (Ms. Elaine Parks) encouraged me to enter teacher leadership and to pursue the National Board Certification process. The National Board process changed my life! It inspired me to become a teacher leader.

Thanks to my former school principals (Monica Smith and Randi Scott-Howard) and my current school principal, Dr. Keyundah Coleman, John P. Freeman Optional School, and Memphis-Shelby County Schools.

To the dynamic duo in the school office, Mia Dodson and Tina Holiday, thank you for the countless times you have helped me; you two are truly irreplaceable.

To my National Board Professional Teaching Standards family, you are remarkable, and you continue to show the world how National Board-Certified Teachers are game changers who transform students' lives. Every child deserves to be taught by an accomplished teacher!

To National Science Foundation: thanks for allowing me to make history as the first and only teacher leader to serve on the Education and Human Advisory Committee.

Special thanks to my contributors (Stephen Ritz, Martha Mcleod, Wendy Turner, Michael Dunlea, Michaal Pope, Sergio De Alba, Claudine James, Majorie Brown, Carlandra Miller, and Claudine James). You are truly inspirational! I am so excited to share your amazing stories with the world!

To my former and current students, thank you for inspiring me to become a teacher leader. You make me enjoy teaching. I will continue to make an impact in student lives each day.

Finally, thanks to the many individuals who are committed to changing the lives of students around the world through the spirit of teacher leadership! You are simply the best!

Meet the Author

Melissa Collins is an elementary school teacher in Memphis, TN, where she is constantly amazed by her students' curiosity about the world around them. Her classroom is her "Happy Place," where she enjoys working with her bright, brilliant, urban students. In her classroom, she promotes scholars that create change in the world through problem-solving. Her entire teaching career has been at John P. Freeman Optional School, right in the very community where she was raised.

She is an expert in teacher leadership and voice, and she is an advocate for global learning, STEM education, and high standards for all students. She believes STEM is for all and collaborates with several organizations to promote and advocate for STEM. She also is the first and only teacher to serve on the National Science Foundation (NSF) Directorate for Education and Human Resources Advisory Committee. She is currently the co-chair for the National Science Teacher Association/Shell Award.

To help ensure that all children have access to caring and committed teachers, she has mentored several teachers through the National Board process. She is a proud National Board-Certified Teacher in Early Childhood Education. She serves as a board member for National Board Professional Teaching Standards. She is a founding member of the National Board Network of Accomplished Minority Educators. To promote higher standards, she has served on the Student Achievement Partners Advisory Board.

Melissa believes in bridging policy and practice and has been a fellow in several policy fellowships such as America Achieves, TN-Teach Plus, and TN-Hope Street group. She has advised policymakers and educational leaders on how to support students and teachers with a focus on equity among our marginalized students. She has been featured on NBC Nightly News for promoting racial harmony and desegregating her classroom.

Melissa has traveled as an NEA Foundation Global Fellow to Brazil and South Africa. She has been recognized as a Maverick Teacher, and she was invited to the Agastya Foundation in India, where she collaborated with other educators to create a curriculum for the children in India.

Melissa has been the recipient of several awards and honors, including Amazon Future Engineer Teacher of the Year, National University Award, Harriet Sanford Award, National Board Fellowship Program, the Global Teacher Prize Finalist (Top 50), the Queen Smith Award, the Stephen Sondheim Award, the Horace Mann Award for Teaching Excellence, the Presidential Award for Excellence in Science Teaching, the National Science Teaching Association (NSTA) Sylvia Shugrue Award, NSTA/ Shell Urban Development Award, and the West Tennessee Teacher of the Year. She was also inducted into the National Teacher Hall of Fame in 2020.

She received her bachelor's degree in early elementary education at Murray State University. She went on to earn a master's in education in 2005, a specialist of education certification in district-level administration in 2008, and a Ph.D. in district-level administration in 2011 from the University of Southern Mississippi.

PART 1

What Is a Teacher Leader?

1

The Road to Teacher Leadership

To be a true leader, you have to be able to turn your vision into a reality.

Going through the National Board Professional Teaching Standard (NBPTS) process altered my view about teacher leadership. Before then, I didn't understand what the term "Teacher Leadership" meant for me or anyone else.

When I entered the profession, I saw myself as only a teacher. I worked in my classroom to ensure students learned, and I collaborated with families and colleagues. I would only interact with the principal when necessary. The classroom was my playground to create a fun learning environment for students.

Then came the National Board Certification; this was the start of my teacher leadership journey. As part of the training certification process, I had to complete a portfolio entry that encouraged me to lead *outside* my classroom walls. This was new for me.

At the time I was pursuing this certification, I was also pursuing an advanced degree because I thought that was the only way to lead in a school setting. As I began looking for ways to lead outside the classroom, I quickly realized that I did not need another degree to be a leader. Instead, I could lead right from my very own classroom, school building, or even our national Capitol building (more on this later). I came to understand teacher leadership as leading in spaces that would create change for our most

DOI: 10.4324/9781003229537-2

vulnerable students. Teacher leaders everywhere make possible the dreams of their students, community, and school.

I recently enjoyed talking to my colleague Claudine James about why she is a teacher leader. Here is what she had to say: "Teaching is not my job; I love it too much to give it such a demeaning title. It's my passion, my motivation, and my reward. Reward? Yes, reward. Each of us should leave a legacy when we leave this earth, a dash, between the year we are born and the year we die. What we do with and in our life is our 'dash.' Being an educator rewards me with a great and lasting legacy. Well, only if I'm an effective educator, and by no means do I strive to be anything other than that. I have to 'be the change [I] want to see in the world.'"

Claudine continues to say, "But does the legacy stop with me, or does it continue? It must continue, not only in my students, but also in my current coworkers and future teachers as well. Our profession is necessary for any other profession to succeed. I feel it is my mission to instill this message in all educators. I am zealous in recruiting and inspiring qualified individuals to join the teaching profession as well as keeping dedicated educators in the education field. It's up to us as educators to 'be the change [we] want to see in the world.' I am dedicated to being a teacher leader because I want to inspire others to see the rewards of being an educator and join this noble profession."

Claudine is spot on. It is imperative for teacher leaders to commit to changing the world for the benefit of our students. The key to doing so is found on the road to teacher leadership. I hope this chapter inspires you to take the next step to build your career and leave a legacy of transformational teacher leadership.

In this book, I will share a few stories with you. Some of the stories are from my own career, and others are about successful teacher leaders I have had the pleasure of working with over the years. Through these stories, you will see critical elements of our paths to teacher leadership.

My teaching journey has not been without hardships. As you know, being a teacher is not easy. I have had many things happen that made me cry, but also many things that have made me jump for joy. At the age of 24, I started teaching while pregnant with my son. To increase my income, I had to take a second job. This weighed on me heavily when trying to be a successful teacher. When I entered my classroom for the first time, I remember being a little nervous, and I did not want to fail. Despite the rough days, I kept trying and would not give up. Often I would call my dad, an educator himself. He always told me what I needed to hear to keep going.

Over the course of my twenty-plus years of teaching, I have made some mistakes, but I learned through those mistakes. As I kept trying to improve, I slowly moved further down the road to teacher leadership.

As I did so, my classroom became an adventure. My students begin to learn, and I knew I was doing my part. Seeing these results, I decided that I could write my own narrative. I created innovative programs and events. The community started to notice my work, and they supported me. I began to put myself out there. I pursued and achieved National Board certification, and it changed my life. I started to pursue other leadership roles as well, and people began to hear my story. I've since traveled the world helping others learn and teach.

I tell you my story because I know that yours can be just as exciting. The tools I discuss in this book have turned the nervous, stressed, and inexperienced woman that I was into a fulfilled teacher who is now making lasting changes in the lives of her students and other educators. The following stories are a few examples of the impact walking the road to teacher leadership has enabled me to have.

Raniya

I was Raniya's second-grade teacher at John P. Freeman Optional School many years ago. Even at her young age, she was a remarkable student-leader who had a drive to learn science, and she especially loved writing. I was not surprised by Raniya's desire at her young age to enter the field of nursing because she wanted to be a nurse/doctor. Years later, Raniya wrote this in her application to nursing school:

> 'What are your hopes and dreams?' This was a writing prompt I was assigned by my second-grade teacher, one of the most influential people of my life thus far. My teacher served not only as my educator, but also as my mentor, my inspiration and a role model, even to this day. She not only supported my dreams but would remind me of my potential daily. As an eight-year-old, I dreamed to be a doctor one day and hoped to be successful at saving lives.

Gerita

One of my third-grade students, Gerita, was very quiet, so I provided her with a journal to record her thoughts. In reading her journal with her, I discovered that she wanted to play basketball and run track. At that time, I was the current middle school girls' basketball and track team coach for grades 6–8. When she was in the 4th grade, I allowed Gerita to practice with both the middle-school basketball and track teams until she could officially try out in middle school. I knew that, by playing sports, she would learn how to interact and work with others. Gerita went on to run track and play basketball. She played basketball until she finished high school, just as I did in school.

Gerita blossomed from this shy girl to a vibrant and successful student. As her teacher, I would implement inquiry-based learning experiences to spark critical thinking and creative skills; I wanted her to continue growing and exploring her passions. She expressed to me that she also dreamed of becoming a nurse, and she and I continued to talk throughout the years.

In a nomination letter, she wrote, "Long after my time [at John P. Freeman], I return often to see Dr. Collins. She continues changing lives. She has continued to change mine as she checks in with me from time to time, ensuring that I am on the path toward my goal of becoming a nurse. Thanks to Dr. Collins,

I am a proud graduate of Middle Tennessee State University and am on my way to nursing school." Currently, Gerita is living her dream as a nurse.

Civil Rights Advocacy

While teaching a unit around the Civil Rights Movement one year, I decided to have my students bring the signs they created in class to the National Civil Rights Museum on what would have been Dr. King's 88th birthday. I took them on my day off, and my dad, son, and I arrived at the museum ready for my students to showcase their protest signs. Because I did not have permission to protest, the security guard asked me to have the students put down their signs.

The parents, students, and I were disappointed. However, I did not contact the office to ask for their permission. To prevent my students feeling discouraged, with the permission of the security guard, the students were able to walk with their signs through the museum. They were so excited, and they were photographed throughout the museum.

Several years passed, and I reached out to the museum to formally ask about my students leading a demonstration march. The museum was happy to assist me and partnered me with Dory Lerner. That year, my students led the first Children Demonstration March at the Civil Rights Museum on what would have been Dr. King's 90th birthday. They dressed in their best attire the same way marchers did during the Civil Rights era. Some of the students were nervous and started to cry. I told my babies this is the day that they march like Coretta and Dr. Martin Luther King to change the world.

"Hold your head up high and march my babies!" I told them. At that, I wanted to cry because my babies were promoting kindness in the world with their signs. They dried their eyes and marched proudly. Coretta and Dr. King would have been proud. They proceeded to march in front of the Lorraine Motel, the building where Dr. King was assassinated. There were thousands of spectators. This event left a lasting impression on many of my students and on the community at large. Dory Learner has continued to support my classroom instruction.

Physics at the Carnival

Carnival Physics was an invention I came up with to teach students about physics using carnival rides. As you can imagine, it was no small undertaking. I called on several stakeholders to assist with the event. Rising Sun Outreach Ministries, under the leadership of Pastor Aaron Campbell, allowed us to use their gym. I met with my colleagues to discuss how we would integrate the program. Some of the teachers were pursuing National Board certification at the time, and they needed to understand how to collaborate and lead inside the classroom and outside in their community, so they helped support the event.

We invited the police department, a baseball team mascot, and a radio personality. The baseball team wanted a small fee, but I told them that I did not have any money, only a dream to host this event for my community. They agreed to do it for free! The radio personality was unsure about participating since he did not know if he could aid the event. After a long conversation, I convinced him that he could motivate students to pursue STEM and talk a little bit about force and motion. He could follow our lead during the program.

I also went to local businesses for funds to purchase giveaways and food. I talked to two vendors who donated rides to the event. On the Saturday of the event, over a hundred people showed up, and the event was thrilling! Several parents thanked me for hosting the event. They said they were motivated to have their child enter a STEM pathway. The radio personality told me that he was surprised by how the event turned out. He was glad that he participated, and he continued to support events that I led until his death. Several of the teachers accomplished National Board certification, and I was glad to be their mentor in the process.

A Dissertation Committee

I have been able to support my fellow teachers in number of ways over the years. One of the more unique experiences happened when a teacher asked me to be on her dissertation committee for her Doctorate of Education (Ed.D.). I was nervous because I had never been on a committee of that magnitude. I presented her with my curriculum vitae, and she presented it to the university. They allowed me to be on the committee.

The teacher's research was on reading, and I enjoyed collaborating with the committee and the teacher. The day she defended her dissertation, I was elated to be in the room because I was supporting an educator on her educational journey. After the teacher finished presenting and exited the room so we could deliberate, it felt good to discuss the educator's accomplishments and reward her with her doctorate.

Field Experiences

Years ago, Michael Dunlea and I attended the KIND Foundation Summit. We were invited to share our story about using Emaptico, a free virtual exchange platform, and discuss how his all-white New Jersey class and my all-black Tennessee class interacted with each other. We talked about how we used technology to desegregate the classrooms.

After we finished speaking, we were each surprised with a $5,000 grant. Daniel Lubutzey, founder and CEO of KIND Foundation, made me cry that day. I used funds to take a few students, parents, and a new teacher on a trip. It was Emma's first time flying. We toured the historical sites of Philadelphia and New York. My students also attended their first Broadway Show, *The Lion King*. In addition, my students were able to surprise their buddies during a professional development session for the New Jersey teachers. It was an emotional interaction for the teachers, students, and families. Emma told a group of teachers and families, "You don't have to be the same race to be friends."

The rest of the money went to purchase books for the primary grade teachers at my school, a field trip for my students to tour the National Civil Rights Museum, and a surprise buffet lunch at a Corky's Ribs & BBQ restaurant. These and other field experiences have helped my students to be engaged in high-quality learning opportunities.

> *As I hope you've seen from these stories, teacher leadership impacts many groups of people. Most importantly, it helps individual students. It also touches parents, stakeholders, administrators, the community, and other educators. In a time when good teachers are in short supply and quitting every day, it has never been more important for people like you and me to learn what teacher leadership is all about.*

What Is Teacher Leadership?

Throughout this book, we will cover many qualities of teacher leaders. But the truth is, you probably already have a sense for who they are. Though not easy to emulate, teacher leaders can be easily recognized. You may even associate with a teacher leader on a daily basis! As you read the following qualities, ask yourself if any teachers you know come to mind.

- ◆ Teacher leaders are passionate about their students. Along with that passion, they find ways to address barriers (i.e. diversity, equity, and inclusion) that affect their students' lives.
- ◆ Teacher leaders know how imperative it is to create a culture of excellence for their students and the school community. They are confident in their instruction, and they expand their reach outside the classroom walls to support students, the community, and the profession.
- ◆ Teacher leaders work to diversify the profession and they advocate for teachers and students of color. They know the importance of students of color seeing professionals in and out their buildings that look like them.
- ◆ Teacher leaders lead from the classroom. They recognize that the classroom is where teachers discover their narratives and where their stories are filled with failures and successes.

- Teacher leaders enhance their pedagogical knowledge and acknowledge the importance of continual learning and discovering and implementing effective teaching techniques.
- Teacher leaders create synergistic relationships within their school community and beyond. They desire to be successful, and they know that they cannot do the work in silos.
- Teacher leaders are action-oriented self-starters. When they see an opportunity to create change, they work diligently with other professionals, businesses, and organizations to make those changes happen.
- Teacher leaders make sacrifices for the greater good, and their reward is seeing how their leadership has changed the lives of their students, their colleagues, and the profession. Although they readily give up comfort for the benefit of others, they also find balance in doing so.
- Teacher leaders guide their colleagues because they want them to advance as well. They understand that teaching is challenging and requires a great deal of work and that it is essential to build the leadership capacity of other teachers for students to succeed. They know that the more teacher leaders that are produced, the more effective the school system will be for our students.
- Finally, teacher leaders persevere through challenges, and they continue to commit themselves to student advancement. They are not afraid to try new things or take on daunting tasks because they know that there is a risk involved in whatever they do. Accolades are appreciated, but teachers find true gratification in seeing their work bring about systemic change.

Have you thought of a colleague or friend in the profession who sounds like a teacher leader? You'll learn more about what makes teacher leaders tick and how to become one in subsequent chapters. One of the most telling traits of teacher leaders is that they go above and beyond the call of duty for the profession and their individual students.

Why Are Teacher Leaders Important?

As fellow teacher leader Majorie Brown told me, "Teachers are often referred to as the backbone of society. As expressed by the University of the People, 'They give children purpose, set them up for success as citizens of our world, and inspire in them a drive to do well and succeed in life. The children of today are the leaders of tomorrow, and teachers are that critical point that makes a child ready for their future.'"

She continued to say, "I think teachers provide stability in a child's life. A teacher can inspire a child to think about a particular career path, and a caring teacher can assist a child overcome self-esteem issues and traverse a difficult time in their life. Teachers are important role models, as people, as community leaders, as careers. I also think teachers can facilitate the discussions and actions that lead to critical thinkers, activists, global citizens and change makers. If teachers transcend themselves and get involved in community issues, pupils will as well, and take them seriously. This will enable them to see they can make a positive difference in society, be it alleviating poverty or tackling discrimination."

That is our goal as teacher leaders: to create change in ourselves and in our students. Teacher leaders are desperately needed. As another colleague of mine, Stephen Ritz, says, "We (teacher leaders) are the ones that [students] are waiting for."

Choose Your Pathway to Leadership

Are you wondering how to get involved in teacher leadership? Teacher leadership can happen at many levels and in any position you may hold. There is no correct entry point. When I work with teachers who aspire to become leaders, I inform them that everyone is different, and they must consider what they do well or what they want to do well. Just as students are provided with differentiated learning experiences, professional teachers need the same thing!

As you reflect, think about what type of leader you want to be. Maybe you want a formal title or an informal title, and that is fine; you can be a life-changing teacher leader in any capacity. It is essential to find your niche while considering the impact that you want to make in your career. It can take place at the school level or outside the school. When selecting a leadership role, I suggest choosing something that you enjoy and do not mind leading out in. To give you an idea of the many ways you can put the skills you'll learn in this book to work, here are a few ways to lead inside or out of your building.

Informal Leadership Roles

These leaders do not have formal titles but work to advance instruction or the profession in meaningful ways both inside and outside of school. Other educators recognize the leaders' work. Here are a few examples of informal leadership roles that teacher leaders are found in.

- **Blogging and social media:** teachers write blog post or post on social media to share their practices or impact policy.
- **Participation in school board meetings:** teachers attend school board meetings to advocate for the profession or students, or they can be present to share their support for an educational issue.
- **Inviting policymakers into your classroom**: teachers invite policymakers to their classrooms to share and showcase their experiences firsthand.
- **Organizing school support with community organizations:** teachers reach out to community partners to aid in school activities, projects, or programs.
- **Trip organizers:** teachers plan field experiences for students, so they can connect learning to the content being taught.
- **Curriculum designer:** teachers create curriculum that aligns with lesson plans to bring their creative and innovative ideas to the classroom.
- **Informal mentoring/coaching:** teachers work with new or colleagues that need support in or outside the classroom.
- **Data analyzer:** teachers analyze data for their students. They look at the trends and adjustment to their practice if needed.

Formal Leadership Roles

Other times, teacher leaders are found with formal appointments or titles, usually selected by other leaders within the school or through volunteering. Their work inspires others at different levels.

- **Task forces with the Department of Education or school districts:** teachers serve on various task forces to advise or make educational recommendations.
- **Curriculum or assessment developer:** teachers create curriculum to support students' academic growth. They also design or provide feedback for assessments.
- **Fellowships (local, state, or national level):** teachers join various types of fellowships to receive training in order to change the educational landscape. The type of fellowships varies based on roles.
- **Sport coaches:** teachers coach sports to help students' social, emotional learning.
- **Academic coaches:** teachers support their peers' instructional practices. They also provide feedback.
- **Club or cheer sponsors**: teachers sponsor clubs and the cheer teams to help with the schools' climate.
- **Grade-level team leaders:** teachers lead their team and host meetings to ensure their team and students are successful. They maintain records of their meetings and report minutes to the administration team.
- **School representatives**: teachers represent their schools at different levels to ensure their school is present and represented. Some representatives go through an election process. The faculty votes for their represented. They report back pertinent information to the school body.
- **Department chairs:** they lead their department by ensuring the department meet to discuss academics and needed support for the department and students.
- **Committee members:** teachers serve on committees to represent teachers' perspectives.

Summary

There are many places from which to start your journey to becoming a teacher leader, and you as a teacher can decide how you want to lead inside or outside the classroom. What matters most is that you start! Teacher leadership is integral to any successful school or community, and teacher leaders are needed now more than ever. If you work to lead out in your classroom, school, and community and don't give up, you will bless the lives of countless others and enact a powerful change in the world.

Stop and Reflect

- ◆ How do you lead inside or outside of school?
- ◆ Why are teacher leaders essential in schools?

2

The Goal, Not the Role

It's not about being a leader; it's about your goals as a leader.

Trying harder to "be a leader" can sometimes be counterproductive. Teacher leaders are not leaders without the people they serve. Although the end goal on the road to teacher leadership may appear nebulous and distant, there are practical guideposts that confirm you're headed in the right direction. These guideposts are what I call "leadership values," and this chapter covers the most important ones.

Following Your Passion

Teacher leaders desire to be creative inside and outside their classroom walls. They want to make a difference, and that is why they strive to be teacher leaders. Their passion fuels their innovation.

Successful teachers find things that intrigue them, and they connect with what they love. That love and excitement come through to their students, making a profound difference in the classroom. Stakeholders are also moved by passionate teachers who love what they do.

Teacher leaders have the willingness to do what is vital for the students and the profession. They strive to do what is essential for themselves, too. They evaluate programs, standards, and their community to create opportunities for their students.

DOI: 10.4324/9781003229537-3

They understand that students' trajectories in school depend in part on their creativity. They want their students' future to be bright, so they create opportunities to help their students to flourish.

Teacher leaders know that the curriculum serves as a blueprint that depicts what content or topics are taught to students. They see the curriculum as a gateway to instill their passion in their classroom. They follow their passion because they want to enjoy what and how they teach. They value teacher autonomy and find authentic ways to insert their passion into their work.

Following their passion often leads teachers to dream big and leaves them determined to make their dreams a reality. They truly focus on what is best for students.

Bringing passion into your work can happen in simple ways. For instance, my urban students lack exposure to STEM careers, and minorities around the country are not well represented in STEM fields. I have a passion for student achievement and STEM, so to capture student interest, I allowed my students to wear white lab coats in class as STEM professionals. When they put on their lab coats, they were happy, smiling, and empowered! Several of my students have informed me that they feel and look like scientists. They also say that their lab coats change how they see themselves in the future.

Through inspirational instruction, students become creatively inspired by the teacher leaders' enthusiasm. Teacher leaders dream big for their students, and their creative spark lights a fire of inquiry in their students. The students enjoy the teacher leaders' innovative ideas because the students find joy in the teacher leaders' passion. They cannot wait to share their experiences from class with their peers and families.

Teacher leaders' passions inspire students to take academic risks and excel in the classroom. Students gain interest in the core subject due to how the teacher leaders engage issues with the students. Teacher leaders cannot fake their passion with their students. But when that enthusiasm is genuine, students feed off it.

Teacher leaders value inspiring the next generation of leaders. When teacher leaders are passionate about a particular topic, they constantly seek to enhance and improve their pedagogical knowledge. Pedagogical knowledge is essential to teacher leaders since it permits them to know more about their craft. They continuously discover ways to incorporate their passion into lessons. Their imagination is the pure driver of their love.

If you want to start moving toward teacher leadership, follow your passion. If you're not passionate about what you do, then you may have strayed from the road to teacher leadership and need to make an adjustment.

Knowing Your Purpose

Closely related to passion is purpose. Teacher leaders know how important it is to have a purpose in their careers—not just to make money. In many ways, having a sense of purpose also makes you more passionate about what you do. Teacher leaders keep going strong because they have a love for children and education. They want to see their children become better learners because they want to make a difference in the lives of their students.

Teacher leaders see teaching as their calling. They enjoy teaching, and they know that they are meant to lead. For example, one of my colleagues left the business sector to pursue an education degree because of her love for continued education and the opportunity to profoundly impact the lives of children as opposed to staring at a spreadsheet all day, every day. She wasn't satisfied with the purpose her business job gave her and found a more fulfilling purpose to life in teaching.

Even though teaching can be overwhelming (and often is), teacher leaders continue to press forward because they know why they entered the profession and hope to make a difference. Teacher leaders seldom get tired of dealing with education issues because doing so is connected to their purpose. The educational system goes through so many changes in the course of a teacher's career, but teacher leaders' love for teaching never wavers; they always enjoy working with kids.

It has been said that some teachers are "trained," and some teachers are "called." If teachers see their work as training, they only want to do what they have been trained to do. They operate in robot mode. However, if they see it as a calling, they teach because they want to. Because of their calling, teacher leaders do not focus on one just part of the children they teach, but have consideration for the whole child—physical, social, emotional, and cognitive. Teacher leaders want to be at work on time. They don't mind coming early or staying late because they want to do what it takes for children to be successful. After all, it's their purpose, and living one's purpose brings fulfillment.

Have you found your purpose? Are you living it? If you are, you're more a teacher leader than you may think.

Promoting Student Achievement

Teacher leaders want their students to become and achieve. After all, isn't that the main goal of education? Teacher leaders understand that a big part of becoming and achieving is academic success; succeeding in the classroom lays a strong foundation for succeeding in life. Teacher leaders accelerate their students learning to perform at the highest levels since they know their students' potential. They encourage students to set short and long-term goals, knowing that goals permit students to work in a targeted area.

Teacher leaders continue to follow up with students to discuss their plans to celebrate small and significant accomplishments along the way. By doing so, teachers become more than instructors: they become mentors. Teacher leaders understand that students are more than "numerical beings" who need to be prepared for state exams. While working within the appropriate boundaries, teacher leaders do what they can to broaden their students' view of the world. They want to create students that are inquisitive and strive to be change agents.

Teacher leaders also value the students' voices and encourage them to speak out and take a stand on issues inside and outside the classroom. They provide students with opportunities to advocate through real-world experiences. When students engage in authentic learning experiences, they change their attitudes and perspectives due to exposure. This is one form of becoming and achieving that is just as important as mastering academic skills.

Teacher leaders strive to help students reach their fullest potential because they value them as unique individuals.

If your students are growing, learning, and achieving, then your job will be joyful, and you'll know you're walking the path of a teacher leader.

Powerful Relationships

During my over twenty years of teaching, I have discovered that I am best able to support students when I invest in powerful relationships with all stakeholders. I have especially enjoyed working with my colleagues for the benefits of education, encouraging and guiding students in the right direction. For instance, Micheal Dunlea, a decorated teacher from New Jersey, and I collaborated on several projects. We developed teacher partnership during our time with America Achieves, an educational policy fellowship. Often, we would speak on the phone about our career aspirations.

I was drawn to Michael's love for children and how he wanted to make a difference in kids' lives. I was also intrigued by his wealth of knowledge and his passion for wanting to create change for himself. One of the projects we did together was to bring our two classes together for the first time (this has since become a reoccurring event) in 2018 to promote racial harmony. His class is all white, and my class is all black. Back then, our primary goal was to spark empathy, curiosity, and creativity regarding cultural differences. We were featured on Lester Holt's NBC Nightly News because we used technology to desegregate our classrooms. This project—and its impact on students and observers—would not have been possible without the professional and powerful relationship I formed with Michael.

Teacher leaders understand the value of relationships, and they seek to collaborate with a variety of stakeholders to maintain success. They know that it is essential to work with others to spur student achievement, improve school communities, and nurture personal growth. Teacher leaders enjoy collaborating with educators who share their same passions; it makes it enjoyable to collaborate on projects and programs together.

Teacher leaders do not just collaborate on one assignment and consider their work done. They continually build and strengthen relationships as they network for the benefit of their students, sharing insights and best practices as they do so. They value the expertise of other individuals because they know they can learn from others. They also know each other's strengths and weaknesses, so they become the perfect team to accomplish a task. They truly value the support that they receive from these relationships, and they are eager to give it as well.

Teacher leaders don't exist in vacuums. They are well connected to powerful teachers and influencers who inspire them and provide means to realize their dreams. If you're walking the road to teacher leadership alone, you're doing it wrong.

Teacher Service

Teacher leaders provide a plethora of services to others. Rather than clocking out after presenting their lessons, they go the extra mile to support the profession, students, and their students' families. Teacher leaders are willing to—and often do—work outside their contract hours to ensure students' success. They are in the profession to change lives. They offer support through their time and knowledge by creating life-changing events, and even by purchasing items such as food and clothing for students in need.

Teacher leaders spearhead events that bring people together to celebrate, learn, and showcase the school community. This doesn't mean that they do all the work themselves—a sure recipe for burnout. No, they *lead* by collaborating with stakeholders to assist with the events or programs because they know it takes support to plan and deliver a successful event. They also invite students to join in the festivities and invite their families to school for dinner or lunch.

Early in my career, I implemented a program called, "Date with Dad." Fathers were invited to have lunch with their children at school. During lunch, the dads received resources on how to support their children at home. It was my goal to increase the number of fathers who interact with their children's education.

What services do you want to provide to your school community? Teacher leaders provide services that extend far beyond the classroom and serve students where they need it most. Teacher leaders must strive to be loyal and dedicated to the students that they serve. They love the teaching profession and joyfully answer the call to sacrifice and serve.

Professional Learning Experiences

Teacher leaders are lifelong learners, and they know it is essential to keep current with educational trends. Teacher leaders know that professional learning experiences make them more valuable as experts. The more they learn, the more they can convey and share ideas with their students, peers, and the school community. Professional learning is vital in any career, and teacher leaders recognize the importance of continuous professional growth. These experiences expose teacher leaders to the world of accomplishments for themselves and the profession.

Teacher leaders are eager to keep current and relevant with best practices and policies. The more exposure teacher leaders get, the more they want to share with stakeholders. They pride themselves on becoming experts in the field and more and more effectively fulfilling their purpose. They have a goal to showcase their wealth of knowledge through sharing, demonstrating, and modeling. Ultimately, their goal is to broaden their own horizon, just as they hope to broaden the horizons of their students.

If you are on a quest for continual improvement, and if that quest regularly brings you to professional learning experiences, then you're passing another guidepost on your journey to become the best teacher leader you can be.

Summary

Teacher leaders value several things for the benefit of the profession. They focus on their principles to create positive change among their students and their school communities. Following your passion, knowing your purpose, promoting student achievement, building powerful relationships, serving, and participating in professional learning experiences are guideposts on the road to success in teacher leadership.

Stop and Reflect

- ♦ How do your passion and purpose influence what you value as a leader?
- ♦ What attributes do you wish you had to make you a better leader?

3
Teacher Sighting

You can't succeed if you don't love what you do and make that love contagious.

Based on what you know about teacher leaders, have you ever seen one doing his or her amazing work? Did it make you curious about learning more about that teacher's innovative classroom techniques? The best teachers don't mind sharing with the world how much they love their careers and students. I enjoy discovering great educators doing great work for students. Throughout my career, I have been on several "teacher sightings" (as I affectionately call them) and spotted many dedicated, creative teachers doing worthwhile work. The most obvious thing about these teachers is that when they unleash their genius and are doing their best work, everyone around can see that they are doing something they were born to do.

These teacher sightings provided me with an opportunity to identify some of the best and brightest educators around. I learned from their best practices, and I applied what they taught me. I have spotted teacher leaders in diverse locations such as on Twitter, at conferences, on-site visits, or in fellowships that I have joined, to name a few.

I suggest you go on your own teacher sightings and observe the teachers who are masters at what they do. Personally, through

DOI: 10.4324/9781003229537-4

going on these teacher sightings myself, I observed some commonalities in each of the teacher leaders I met:

- ◆ They love what they do.
- ◆ They focus on what is best for their students and communities.
- ◆ They step out of their comfort zones to be the best educators that they can be for all students.
- ◆ They build and maintain a reputation for themselves.
- ◆ They receive multiple recognitions for their innovative ideas.
- ◆ They look at their identity and their students' identities to be the teacher that they wanted as a child to implement impactful change.
- ◆ They don't mind sharing their innovative ideas with others.

The authentic ideas of these teacher leaders made me want to do more for my students and the school community. In fact, their ideas have spilled over into my classroom. I have to admit part of my success to these leaders, as do most other successful educators—teachers borrow ideas from colleagues. Haven't you borrowed a few ideas from others? I have done that in my career several times, but I put my own spin on it to make it work for my students and me.

This chapter is dedicated to all the extraordinary teachers out there who create worthwhile opportunities for their students. You showed others and me that it is commendable to be different and work outside districts and states' blueprints, instead of choosing to be teacher leaders doing extraordinary things. Teachers become teacher leaders through the inspiration that comes from watching other teacher leaders in action. From my own life, my classroom continues to be "Our Happy Place" for me and my students because of the shining examples I have observed over the years.

For the rest of the chapter, I introduce eight phenomenal teacher leaders who you will hear from throughout this book: Stephen Ritz, Marjorie Brown, Wendy Turner, Micheal Dunlea, Serigo De Alba, Martha Mcleod, Carlandra Miller, and Claudine James. You will learn how I met them and how they inspired me as a teacher leader. I hope these extraordinary individuals inspire you to create magical moments for your students. I also hope that they inspire you as you go on your journey of teacher leadership.

Are you ready?

Meet Stephen Ritz

Stephen Ritz is known as "The Teacher Farmer" around the world. I met Stephen in Dubai when I was up for a million dollars. I was a Top 50 finalist for the Global Teacher Prize, and Stephen was a Top 10 finalist the previous year. In hearing Stephen's story about his community and how he wanted to assist his community in living healthier through farming, I was intrigued by how he created an indoor garden within his school.

After hearing him speak, I instantly wanted to learn more about his "Passion, Purpose, and Hope" for his Bronx community. Additionally, I remembered him because of the cheese hat that he wears. Stephen has encouraged me to do more for myself and my school community. I hope to follow his example and engage my students in learning more about living things. I am also inspired to solve more problems in my community due to Stephen Ritz. If you hear him speak, you will embrace the positive energy that he displays and his love for his students.

Learn More about the Teacher Farmer

Who Is Stephen Ritz?

"I am the son of an immigrant. I am an accidental teacher, never intended to be a teacher. And the joke in my family was going to be who would graduate first, my dad or me? But my mom was a teacher, and I got into the profession sideways. I'm still hoping to be in the NBA, but 45 years later, the Knicks haven't woken up. I am still available. But I always had the ability to connect with people. And the ability to connect with people is at the heart of what teachers do."

"I found out at an early age I had a gift with children, usually the most marginalized and disconnected children as well. That gift has enabled me to grow something greater and change lives not only in my home community, but all around the world."

When Did You Start with the Gardening at Your School?

"I started this after the millennium, right around 2004. I was given a group of children, young people who had come out of jail, and asked to teach science, and I had no science background. It was kind of like setting them and me up to fail. We happened to learn sideways about an opportunity which involves doing some park work. Everybody wanted those children and me out of the school because they were perceived as dangerous. I was considered disruptive. It turned out that those 17 students not only stayed out of jail but went on to rebuild chunks of the city. Also, they helped rebuild New Orleans after Katrina and gave birth to a movement in the South Bronx, with some of the highest unemployment in all of New York City."

"We stand proud. We stand tall. It was literally the opportunity to plant seeds. The thing about farming is you don't go from seeds to harvest without cultivation in the middle. I like to say the thing that I am growing most is community and people."

Why Did You Focus on Farming?

"The most important school supply in the world is food. You can't teach a child who's hungry. You can't teach a child who hasn't eaten in days. Similarly, even for wealthy children, you can't teach a child who's eating junk full of sugar, caffeine, and dumbed down by all these chemical additives. Children will never be well read if they are not well fed, so giving children access to fuel their bodies and their minds when they need it most is one of the most critical acts we can do."

How Are the Students Engaged in Your Program?

"Children love to do things. They love to do things, and they love to be engaged. I believe that no child rises to low expectations. When you set the bar high, children rise to it."

"Our classroom is a farm four stories up in the middle of public housing in one of the oldest buildings in New York City. We grow copious amounts of food, and we do it 365 days a year and with 90% less water and 90% less space. They love taking care of the farm; they love taking care of the fish tank; they love taking care of little things; and they think their job is to come to school and take care of all these things."

"They are really doing reading, writing, math, science, career development, entrepreneur skills, and everything else that is fundamental to living. Every 30 days, we have got tons of food to eat and sell. It works well. It is kind of smoke and mirrors, and I believe the most effective teachers are engaged in some form of project-based learning. Having children believe that they're doing one thing, while they are learning to cooperate, communicate, and collaborate."

How Do Your Students Perform?

"Our students in the poorest congressional district in America and the formerly poorest performing school district in all of New York City outperform their age and race equivalent peers in every single performance indicator. A school that was once developing and not proficient in every single benchmark is now well developed and proficient in every benchmark. We have teachers who come from around the world. My classroom has hosted teachers from 60 countries. I like to say 150,000 of vegetables later. My favorite crop is organically grown citizens, graduates, members of the middle-class children who are going to college, environmental and social justice equity warriors. That is what it's about. Children love coming to school. We have some of the highest attendance rates in all of New York City in one of the most challenged communities."

What Were Some of Your Career Highlights?

"To see the lives changed, farms built, jobs created, and families thriving right here in my home community and around the world is the greatest highlight one could ask for. To have my portrait painted by my hero, Robert Shetterly, for the Americans Who tell the Truth series is the greatest honor one could ask for. I'm particularly proud that our Green Bronx episode of *Growing a Greener World* – Episode 808 – won the first ever Emmy Award for the series and in NYC Department of Education history, forever changing the narrative of the way people see my community is surely up there as is witnessing Green Bronx Machine scale to hundreds of schools and other countries around the world. To have a number-one, best-selling book, *The Power of a Plant* and award-winning documentary, Generation Growth, are accomplishments that I could have never imagined. Being invited to – and installing farms at – the Obama White House with students are also high on the list."

"Greater than awards and honors, my career highlight is the difference I have been able to make in the lives of those I serve. This highlight is due to being able to focus on appreciating my role as a transformative educator. At the center of every decision, I keep in mind that teaching is a gift, not only for students but for teachers who want to make the world better as no other profession can touch as many lives."

Meet Majorie Brown

I met Majorie Brown in Dubai, just like Stephen Ritz. Majorie was a Global Teacher Prize Top 10 during the year I was in the Top 50. In talking to Majorie, I learned that she was a former human rights activist. She believed that it was important that South African students learned South African history. She taught history at an all-girls' school. In 1980, at the height of apartheid, she helped to found an all-girls' school, since she did not want to work in an integrated school. She encouraged students to read to aid with critical thinking through reading. Majorie has introduced reading quizzes to poorly resources schools in South Africa. Majorie is passionate about exposing her students to reading through the use of taking quizzes. Majorie has talked to my students on several occasions, and she has encouraged me to create more historical opportunities for students.

More from the Reading Teacher

When Did You Start?
"About 18 years ago, I introduced the Kids Lit Quiz into South Africa (SA) – this is a high-powered international quiz for age

5–7 year olds who have to answer questions on the last 2000 years of English literature from around the world (see www.kidslitquiz. com). This raised the standard of reading in schools participating around South Africa, but we have a very unequal country in terms of schooling and access to books, so I started another project, Phendulani, where I encouraged well-resourced schools in Kids Lit Quiz to sponsor or support kids in poorly resourced schools. I then lobbied book dealers and publishers for book donations and handed between 12–20 books to under-resourced schools in SA, and based a quiz on these books, called Phendulani Literacy quiz. I work with 127 schools on Kids Lit Quiz, and 150 schools on Phendulani, trying to encourage reading and critical thinking on all levels."

How Are the Students Engaged in Your Unique Setting?

"The students who do either quiz love it, and the excitement of being part of the quiz is evident by the reading levels, as well as the evaluation I do of the quiz with the students around the country each year. When I ask Phendulani kids how the quiz can be improved, they invariably answer, 'With more books.'"

How Have Your Innovative Ideas Helped Your Students Perform?

"The children who participate in Kids Lit Quiz and Phendulani love the thrill and challenge of the reading competition. For Phendulani schools, it means a steady injection of donated books each year. Reading levels have grown enormously, as well as the culture of reading generally in these schools. For Kids Lit Quiz schools, the winning team travels to a world final somewhere in the world to take on national winners from 8 other countries. For a relatively small country of well-resourced readers taking on the UK, Canada, USA, Singapore, Thailand, Australia, China and New Zealand, SA has done pretty well, winning the quiz at least 4 times."

"Another activity I am known for is encouraging knowledge of current affairs through Model United Nation debating. Through this my students have become part of Youth Policy groups at the local university, and three of my students helped draft the youth statement on climate policy for the City of

Johannesburg and were part of the SA Youth Statement on Policy around Climate Action for COP 26. To see such young students become changemakers and sit on the world stage with leaders, Ministers, businesspeople, academics, and hold their own is a sign of how empowered they are through this activity."

"A further activity is the social responsibility which I help coordinate at school. Students partake on a voluntary basis in Monday projects each week, whereby our volunteers work with inner-city orphans and vulnerable children and assist with literacy and numeracy. We combine these activities with worksheets on climate change and combating discrimination, so literacy is a tool for values-based education as well. Our students take part in the international climate action project and were designated as a school of excellence for teaching on climate action this year."

What Were Some of Your Career Highlights?

"I was able to interact and network with inspiring teachers on issues of sustainable development goals, climate action, transformation, history and peace and conflict issues, and also talk on webinars to world leaders, and share practical experiences from my corner of the world. I was also able to stand on the stage of the Mandela 100 Global Citizen concert, with Trevor Noah, one of my heroes and call for people to get involved in change. I also had the opportunity to speak to other great teachers such as Peter Tabichi, for young teachers to hear and be inspired by other role models in education, for National teacher mentoring programs."

Meet Wendy Turner

Wendy is known to me as "The Social-Emotional Teacher." Here is why: At the National Network of State Teacher of the Year (NNSTOY) conference in Orlando, Florida, I spotted Wendy Turner during her TED Talk. She was speaking on how she addressed social-emotional learning. She created an environment where students could articulate their emotions in her class.

Wendy believes that social-emotional learning is "the foundation of learning, the ground floor of the building, and the foundation of the schoolhouse. Without it, the institution crumbles."

By the end of each morning, her students select a bracelet from a red basket that has a powerful question written on it—how are you feeling today? They select a green, yellow, or red bracelet to share their mood. Green bands indicate that they are feeling great and red bands indicate anger or other negative emotions. The bracelets enabled her young students to articulate their feelings. Her students would ask their peers' further questions to understand their classmates' feelings.

As we all know, feelings can change. The kids can change the bracelets throughout the day too. Wendy wore bracelets, too, to model her feelings for her students. Her TED Talk was so compelling that I started following her on Twitter and Facebook. Wendy motivated and inspired me to expose my students to more social and emotional learning opportunities. I have a banner displayed in my room that asks, "How are you feeling today?" Now my students place their numbers by their emotions (e.g., happy, okay, sad, or mad). Wendy and I stayed in contact through social media outlets. We also had an opportunity to travel to South Africa together as Global Fellows with the National Education Foundation. While on that trip, I learned more about Wendy's passion for teaching and learning.

More about the Social-Emotional Teacher

I asked Wendy a few questions about her story and best practices.

When Did You Start?

"I started embracing social-emotional learning right away in my teaching career. I start with direct instruction around empathy, brain science, emotions and feelings, and the language we use in the classroom. I then provide opportunities for students to regulate and manage themselves in various ways and support each other in difficult moments. I have added to my toolkit over the years to enhance my classroom environment and make it student-centered. I have also worked on developing my own SEL skills and core competencies as I believe this is an essential component to powerful and impactful classroom SEL."

How Are the Students Engaged in Your Unique Setting?

"My students are engaged with a human-centered approach that involves active learning about social-emotional skills and academics, collaboration, a real-world lens, honest discourse, and hard work that is nurtured, supported, and facilitated by me. We also hear and listen to each others' stories. By regularly seeking and reviewing feedback from my students, I make constant adjustments to our process and our space. A noisy classroom with ideas, all emotions, and supplies being shared constantly is the norm. During COVID-19 and remote teaching, my heart was broken by not being able to walk among my students. With perseverance and innovation, we figured out ways to "walk with each other" no matter where we were physically located."

How Have Your Innovative Ideas Helped Your Students Perform?

"I find that my students exhibit a high degree of empathy and self-management using my innovative ideas. One day during a collaborative math activity, I noticed a table group working together where one boy was not talking much at all. He started to look upset, and his body position also reflected this mood change. His tablemates were not aware of the change and continued with their discussion of the task. All of a sudden, this student, who was wearing a green bracelet, stomped over to the basket of bracelets in our classroom and changed his green one to a red one. He came back to the table and all of the other students noticed. I then heard one say, 'We need to listen to our friend, I think he's getting mad because we're not talking to him.' I was so proud of ALL of my students in this scenario! One student used our non-verbal system to convey a mood change, and the other students used empathy to realize what was happening and include him in the activity. I didn't have to say a word and they did this on their own."

What Were Some of Your Career Highlights?

"One kind of highlight I would call like, really conventional. It's about being recognized for the work that I've done. My work has been around supporting the whole child and social emotional learning. So being recognized as the 2017 Delaware teacher of the year, the year was absolutely a career highlight and that happened after only six years of teaching. For me, I was a career changer, and it just validated the work that I was doing. The year that I was nominated. At my building level, every single staff member, every nomination was for me, there was no one else that was even mentioned, so that was just incredible validation of all the work I was doing."

Also, she adds, "Other career highlights along those lines include being recognized as a compassion champion by the state of Delaware, also being able to represent Delaware as an NEA Foundation Global Learning Fellow with traveling to South Africa and then bringing ideas around global confidence and global learning back to my classroom in my community."

"Another highlight was being a guest on the Cult of Pedagogy podcast, which is a really big education podcast."

Meet Michael Dunlea

In 2012, I met Michael Dunlea in New York City. We were both in a fellowship called America Achieves. The fellowship had us both in New York for about a week to learn more about policy and teaching. The two of us had an intense conversation on how to help shape education. Michael and I were in this fellowship for three years, so we had plenty of time to learn about each other's passions and purpose in education.

When the fellowship ended, Michael and I remained friends, and we would talk about our next steps in education. In 2017, Michael and I participated in a global project, and we had our classes meet. I noticed his class was all white and my class was all black. We knew we had to do something to promote racial harmony. We used Empatico, a virtual platform to connect our classes. We paired our students with buddies, and they wrote and exchanged gifts with each other.

In collaborating with Michael, I realized he loved global learning. He created several opportunities for our students to engage in global experiences. I gave Michael the name "The Global Teacher." His room is decorated with flags from different countries and substantial development goals. Students are engaged in global projects as he serves as a global ambassador. My class participated in more global projects because of The Global Teacher. Michael inspires me to implement more global learning in my classroom. We hosted a Global Read-A-Thon together where we invited different readers from around the globe to read a selected book from their respective countries.

When Did You Start Your Initiatives?

"I started about five years ago after attending a workshop conducted by another teacher leader named Maryann Wood-Murphy from NJ. She was presenting at an ECET2 conference about teaching with global competencies and fostering global citizenship skills and traits in your students."

How Are the Students Engaged in Your Unique Setting?

"Students are engaged by their interest in connecting with other teachers and students. The learning is organic and authentic, which helps keep their interest high and their performance on target. All the speaking, listening, writing, and reading standards are in play when we are working with another class from some-where in the country or world. Students are driven by curiosity and inquiry. The skills of compare and contrast are so naturally occurring when my students meet other students. My students become leaders and ambassadors of our class, district, state, and country depending on who we are connecting with. The empowerment and responsibility raise their commitment to the learning and therefore increases their engagement."

How Have Your Innovative Ideas Helped Your Students Perform?

"I have been a classroom teacher for 19 years, and 17 of them I have been in the inclusion classroom. This means I have almost always had students with learning differences and Individualized Education Programs (IEPs). This neural diversity setting has led to amazing breakthroughs. Students who have historically struggled in traditional classroom learning environments often tend to excel in the highly engaged global learning environment. They thrive when they get to connect with another student from far away. They suddenly are a person of high interest to another student. They are no longer a struggling student but instead are a leader showing others how to do it. It completely reshapes their self-image as a learner and instills greater confidence and self-esteem. In addition to this, the students regularly outperform their peers on standardized assessments such as the Partnership for Assessment of Readiness for College and Careers (PARCC), Measurement of Academic Progress, MAP, and other district assessments. The authenticity of the learning leads to deeper, more critical thinking and greater understanding that goes beyond what traditional learning would lead to."

What Are Some Career Highlights?

"I have been a finalist for NJ Teacher of the Year the first time I changed my path. It led to many fellowship opportunities and it began me on my leadership journey. The two biggest moments for me were achieving the National Board certification and receiving the Presidential Award of Excellence in Mathematics and Science Teaching."

Meet Sergio De Alba

Now, it is time to meet Sergio, "The Community Garden Teacher."

I met Sergio in Bethesda, Maryland during a National Assessment of Educational Progress (NEAP) Interactive Science Task meeting. Sergio and I were selected to serve on that committee. We had to provide feedback to NEAP on how materials should be presented to students. We both were true advocates for the student population that we served. I learned a lot about Sergio during our time together.

As a Hispanic teacher, Sergio embraces his culture and traditions, and he has worked with many Hispanic students in California.

He told me about the importance of school gardens because of the connection his students have to agriculture. Finding relevant connections to his students inspired and empowered them to want to learn. "Agriculture was an important part of their community," he said, "… it affects the entire region in one way or another. Having this connection was important. If you want to create a successful program, ensure that it is relevant to your students."

I could easily visualize the joy that he exposed to his students. For years, I wished that I could visit his school. When I served as the Chair for the National Science Teacher Association (NSTA) Shell Award, I had the opportunity to finally visit it. In looking at the various gardens, I was amazed at what he had created for his school community. There were rose gardens, pumpkin and cabbage patches, a place for digging artifacts, a stage with a garden, and so much more. He even created areas that had colorful cobblestones. Sergio and his community put a lot of effort into creating an outdoor space for learning. He motivated me to expose my students to living things and to not be afraid to ask for stakeholders' assistance. Because of his innovation, I called him "The Garden Teacher."

More from the Garden Teacher

When Did You Start Your School Garden Project?
"Our School Garden program began in 2001. The idea was initiated by a student to improve the school site and educational success of students."

How Are the Students Engaged in Your Unique Setting?
"Our garden program consists of sixteen gardens throughout the campus. Each garden is designed with a mandated curriculum in mind and provides an avenue to enrich lessons given in any grade. For example, primary students have thematic gardens that focus on the life cycle of plants and animals. Intermediate students are provided an opportunity to learn about farming, business, propagation methods, and a variety of other lessons that focus on knowledge relevant to a farming community."

How Have Your Innovative Ideas Helped Your Students Perform?

"The gardens allow for hands-on enrichment opportunities that enhance the lessons given in the classroom. It is the focus on engagement and empowerment provided by the garden program that has allowed students to learn the required material at a greater pace, and in turn, perform well on state exams."

What Were Some of Your Career Highlights?

Sergio has been recognized as a 2019 Henry Ford Teacher Innovator Award, 2020 National History Teacher of the Year, and inducted into the National Teacher Hall of Fame class of 2022. along with several other honors. However, he says, "Greater than awards and honors, my career highlight is the difference I have been able to make in the lives of those I serve. This highlight is due to being able to focus on appreciating my role as a transformative educator. At the center of every decision, I keep in mind that teaching is a gift, not only for students but for teachers who want to make the world better as no other profession can touch as many lives."

Meet Martha Mcleod

Next, we have Martha, "The Nature Park Teacher." She is from Rockport, Texas and was inducted into the National Teacher Hall of Fame in 2013.

My first time seeing the magnificent Martha Mcleod was on a video. As a chair for the National Science Teacher Association (NSTA)-Shell Award committee, I had an opportunity to watch videos, read applications, and visit three of our finalists' classrooms. In reviewing Martha's application, I could tell that she was a passionate STEM teacher. I was eager to learn more about her birding program—where members observed birds—and also about the school garden she showcased.

When Martha was a finalist for NSTA-Shell Award, I was ecstatic because I could not wait to learn more about her practices. When I entered Martha's class, I saw that she had reptiles, fish, incubators with eggs, and animals mounted to name a few. STEM was alive and vibrant in her classroom. Her students were highly engaged in their learning experiences, and I enjoyed talking to her students.

Her community also loved Martha; everyone supported her work. While walking outside her school, I could not believe that she had created an entire nature park for her school community. The nature park has an array of wildlife and domestic animals. On any given day, birds feast on the feed set out in feeders by students. The campus chickens are always available for treats too, whether that involves a snack of invasive species or an apple core leftover from a student's lunch box. There are rabbits, chickens, flowers, carrots, and man-made ponds, to name a few. She even let me hold a chicken! Martha was devoted to her nature park, and that is why I called her The Nature Park Teacher. Martha inspired me to connect with community partners to implement STEM activities at my school.

Wisdom from the Nature Park Teacher

When Did You Start Your Park?
"I focused on creating gardens at our school so that my students would have access to seeing the beauty of nature. When students are immersed in nature, it has a soothing and calming effect on them. Plus, many of our state standards are covered when students investigate out in the field. I started creating a variety of gardens with kids about 20 years ago. Our aluminum-can recycling program generated funding over the years to purchase enhancements and expand our projects."

How Are the Students Engaged in Your Unique Setting?
"Students actively participate in the maintenance of our many gardens through a 'Garden Core' program. A core group of students serve as team leaders and then train the other students in specialized jobs such as egg gathering, invasive species removal, filling of bird feeders and birdbaths, watering of vegetables, etc."

How Have Your Innovative Ideas Helped Your Students Perform?

"A majority of our students (70%) come from backgrounds of poverty. Many of them have reduced opportunities to build real-world background experience. Our students are able to perform fairly well on state standard assessment and compete with other more affluent districts through our many hands-on learning components."

What Were Some of Your Career Highlights?

Martha is a decorated educator, and she has received several honors such as: 2010 Presidential Awards for Excellence in Mathematics and Science Teaching, 2013 National Teachers Hall of Famer inductee, 2020 Shell Science Teaching Award, and 2021 National Excellence in Teaching about Agriculture Award to name a few.

She shares a few other highlights, "Teacher highlights include the successful vegetable gardens we created where all 700 students are able to grow and sample a variety fresh vegetable.

Another highlight would be the creation of the 2 acres of pollinator/wildlife/cactus gardens, that includes a huge outdoor classroom, which benefits both the students and the wildlife, both current and future for many years to come.

A third highlight would be the formation of the youth birding program I created 12 years ago which has flourished."

Meet Carlanda Miller

Have you ever been to Disney World or Disneyland? I have taken my son to Disneyland on several occasions. Every time I have taken him, he has not wanted to leave, since Disneyland provides families with a magical experience. When I sighted Carlanda Miller ("The Magical Teacher") on Twitter, I was intrigued by her classroom culture and climate. Her room was decorated in a Disney magic theme. She had royal-blue wallpaper, colorful Mickey Mouse silhouettes on the walls and on the floors, bright red curtains, a child-size stage, an oversized castle on the wall, a cozy reading center, and a U-table for small group instructions. Her room was inviting and welcoming for students.

This magical teacher often dresses up in Disney costumes for her students. She has created a magical environment that has caused her to go virtual on three occasions. She spent much of her own personal money to create that fabulous environment for her students, and she does so each and every year. She has inspired me to design a classroom that is welcoming and affirming for my students.

About the Magical Teacher

When Did You Start Making Your Classroom Magical?

"Five years ago, maybe on the first day of school, one of my students came in the classroom probably half throughout the day. She raised her hand and she said that our classroom was so magical. You're the magical teacher! The whole class went crazy, and it gave me chills. It was one of those moments where I will never forget. I asked my boyfriend at the time if I should go with the name 'Magical Teacher.' He said, 'Go for it.' Now I go by The Magical Teacher, and I spread magic in my classroom. The word 'MAGIC' stands for Motivation, Academic Accountability, Goal-Driven, Inquisitive Thinking, and Constant Engagement. I do these five things in my classroom to make it magical. I feel if you do this, your students will be magical. You'll pull their magic out of them. That's where it came from."

How Are the Students Engaged in Your Unique Setting?

"Every student feels welcome, and they actually take very good care of my classroom. The way that people see it online is literally what it looks like at all times. My students take pride in their room. We do a lot of movement, a lot of call responses. So there's really no time for students to not be engaged because we're always moving and using hand gestures to help them to recall concepts. My classroom runs like an oiled machine. The structure is important to me, and I ring a bell to gauge students and get their attention. I have one sound where they know that means to stop and clean up and another sound that means to rotate. They know exactly what to do. In the morning, when they first come in, their morning work is already out. Then I bring them to the carpet. Everything is just structured for the students. I think that's what a lot of kids need in their life—a lot of structure. Also, there is a stage in the room to promote students' voices. Students lead as the teacher. Mickey lanterns are colored coded for differentiated instruction. Magic happens at all times!"

How Have Your Innovative Ideas Helped Your Students Perform?

"I think my students perform very well based on just their belief in themselves. I try to teach students to believe in themselves, that they can do anything they put their mind to. I also teach coping skills. You can study, study, study. But what happens if you don't pass that test? What are you going to do or what happens if you don't get to do this activity that you wanted to do? So I think that what is really important in education is teaching kids what to do when that power does not quite make it."

What Are Some of Your Career Highlights?

Carlanda, "The Magical Teacher" has been a 2017–2018 Teacher of the Year, motivational speaker, and author. She is a lover of Disney, but I am not surprised. Also, she has been on the Kelly Clarkson show on three occasions.

Meet Claudine James

Claudine reached out to me on Messenger to say congratulations. I was elated that she reached out to me when I received the National University Teacher Award. Claudine received the award the previous year. In viewing Claudine's Facebook page, I noticed that she was outgoing, loved her family, liked to cook, and supported educators. On several occasions, she would post messages about other outstanding educators discussing their accomplishments. One time, she highlighted me on her page. I was grateful because sometimes it can be difficult to receive recognition from your peers. This made me follow her page even more.

During the pandemic, I observed her creating grammar lesson videos for her English as a Second Language (ESL) students. She was dedicated to creating several lessons each week. I commended her for finding a way to reach her students during these unprecedented times. Then I noticed her making TikTok videos. She posted on her page that she had at least a million followers. I was very impressed that she had gone viral for her grammar lesson TikTok videos. Technology is a great way to capture the minds of all students. Claudine inspired me to increase my technology use to reach all students. I want to create more visual learning opportunities for students, and I affectionately dub her "The TikTok Teacher."

Viral Thoughts from The TikTok Teacher

When Did You Start Making Videos?
"On December 1, 2020, I started posting grammar lessons on TikTok in order to reach virtual students who weren't watching my videos on YouTube. Just a few months later, I had over 2.7 million TikTok followers from 82 different countries."

How Are the Students Engaged in Your Unique Setting?
"ESL learners have learned basic grammar skills needed for language acquisition, others have received academic refreshers, and many use it to study for tests such as the ACT."

How Have Your Innovative Ideas Helped Your Students Perform?
"Since 2017, my students' reading scores exceeded the district's goal of 60% improving their scores. I work towards overall student achievement, but there are many personal testimonials: 'You helped me to become the BEST writer I could be. I'm very lucky to get a teacher like you.' That was from a student in 2017; she and 13 other students in my 8th-grade class placed in the National Letters About Literature essay contest. Over half went on to pass their AP exams in their sophomore/junior year."

"'Letting us participate in this exhibit was the best thing a teacher has ever done for me,' another student said. She was a phenomenal presenter, impressing all exhibit attendees. Her mother recognized the impact and asked me to continue working with her as a mentor. Our 'partnership' continued throughout her high school years. She graduated #1 in her class, Senior Class, Honor Society, and Beta Club president and received $25,000 in scholarships, and from my nomination, won the city's Outstanding Youth Award. She's currently in college."

"Alex, another student, wrote this to me: 'We've been taught how to be great, successful writers in general, and that can lead us very far in life. I can happily say that I am not alone in being influenced …' The confidence Alex gained in writing in my class allowed him to pass AP exams and receive scholarships. 'How did you know I could read so many books?' he asked. 'I didn't know I could; you believed in me.' My classroom achievement testimonials now extend around the world. On TikTok, I read: 'You helped me learn English!!', 'Your videos helped me to pass the ACT,' and 'I learn more on TikTok than I do in class, thank you, teacher.'"

What Were Some of Your Career Highlights?

Claudine James says, "becoming National Board and ESL certified were two defining moments in her journey of becoming an educational leader. She's won numerous awards included Honored, LifeChanger, Sanford Harmony and the Arkansas TESOL educator of the year. She now states she has a "classroom without walls" as a TikTok educational content creator with over 3 million followers from 87 different countries."

Summary

Teacher sightings can be inspiring to all teacher leaders. They can provide you with insights on how to create a classroom that is inviting to all students and a community that creates positive change. Teacher leaders' students excel academically because they don't focus on numbers but on the development of the whole child. They remember that the child is more than the data. Students will achieve because they enjoy learning from rigorous, novel experiences. When students are engaged in critical thinking, they learn and maintain taught skills/concepts.

Following the example of the best teacher leaders and adapting their best practices to meet the needs of your students will have you creating a reputation of a teacher leader yourself in no time.

Stop and Reflect

- ♦ What do the teacher leaders featured in this chapter have in common? How are they different?
- ♦ What ideas from these teacher leaders do you want to implement in your school?

PART 2

Becoming a Teacher Leader

4

Mentor Matchmaking
How to Find the Perfect One for You

A good mentor will help you bring out your talents that you didn't even realize you had!

Every teacher needs great mentors to encourage them, guide them, and impart wisdom. These mentors are as critical to your success as is everything else. I learned this lesson over my years in the teaching profession through many career-changing experiences. The first step you must take to become a teacher leader is to find your perfect match—a mentor who can show you how.

Assigned the Wrong Mentor

Often teachers are assigned mentors who cannot support them. The mentor and mentee may not share things in common such as the content or grade level they teach, making it difficult for the mentee to grow and thrive when support and guidance are limited. As a result, new teachers are often left in isolation having no one to talk to about their insecurities or lack of understanding and they begin to feel lonely or left out of the school culture and climate.

New teachers are doomed to fail before they become successful; failure is an important part of growth. Because of this,

DOI: 10.4324/9781003229537-6

teachers must find a mentor who can support them inside and outside of the classroom.

I can still remember the day I entered my classroom for the first time—Room 10, a place I'll never forget. I was excited! I was eager to decorate my classroom so that I could give my students a warm welcome. I was also prepared to teach my students at an accelerated rate and produce outstanding students. There was no time for anxiety or doubt. At least, that's what I thought.

The first week of school, however, was full of professional development days. These meetings gave me a limited amount of time to learn about my school, my co-workers and the school's mission, culture, and climate. There was no time for planning, studying the curriculum, or analyzing the textbooks. As a new teacher, I didn't even have time to enter my own classroom for days.

I knew that I needed to have confidence in the students who were getting ready to enter my classroom. As a former athlete, my competitive spirit did not want to fail at being a teacher. My years of playing basketball taught me that I could not be successful if I did not have a sufficient coach to guide my training. When I entered the school building that first day, I knew that I needed a coach to help train me to be the best teacher that I could be inside and outside of my classroom.

To help me on my journey, I was assigned a mentor by the building-level administrator. When I met my mentor, she was friendly and warm, but she did not teach my content, and her classroom was located on the other side of the building. I hardly saw her or received guidance from her.

After a few days of feeling lost and overwhelmed, I knew deep down that if I wanted to survive, I had to find my own mentor. This assigned mentor was not my perfect match. I was on a mission to find the coach who could train and lead me. It would not be easy because a lot of teachers get stuck in isolation themselves, busily trying to survive in their classroom.

On several trips to the teacher lounge, I overheard a particular teacher teaching, Shirley Echols. I could tell her kids were engaged and learning at a high level. Her room was also colorful, bright, and well-decorated. I could tell she had a gift for teaching students, and I admired her hard work and dedication.

Wanting to learn more, I began to eat lunch in this teacher's classroom. Whatever she was doing, I wanted to do it too. As I modeled her teaching methods, my students began to excel, and I had a boost of confidence. I wanted to be a great teacher like her. She tried to turn me away at first because she was not assigned to me, and she wanted me to play by the rules. In this instance, I decided to go against management's policies to get to greatness for my students. When she saw my persistence, she eventually consented.

One of the greatest lessons this mentor taught me was the importance of learning about my students. If I learned about my students' weaknesses and strengths, I could plan accordingly to ensure that they understood the material. She also helped me realize that I had to get my students engaged and motivated to learn if they were to soar to new intellectual heights.

The more time I spent with my mentor, the more I recognized that I was changing and the more I learned who I wanted to become as a teacher. My mentor and I worked well together, and my hypothesis was confirmed that the right mentor would be a bridge to my success.

The Purpose of a Mentor

Every teacher needs a mentor. Why? Mentors play a vital role in building novice teachers' capacities. They support novice teachers in developing a game plan for surviving inside and outside the classroom. Learning about the school's culture and climate is an integral part of learning about stakeholders.

The mentor makes sure that the new teacher establishes a classroom environment conducive to students' learning. They help with setting up the classroom to make sure that it is welcoming for students. They offer suggestions on how to create the right climate to motivate and engage students.

They also provide recommendations on how to present to students, such as how a new teacher writes on the board or communicates with parents. Mentors assist with lesson planning to ensure highly effective lessons are provided to all students.

They offer feedback on lessons and give core content advice. Mentors also share strategies to accommodate different modalities. They provide suggestions on analyzing and adapting to students' strengths and weaknesses and offer feedback based on their observations of classroom lessons, which helps novice teachers make needed adjustments and measure their success.

Most importantly, the mentors follow up with their mentees to check on and balance their growth. They help them establish the best plan for developing into a successful teacher leader. They will support their mentees teachers with planning, provide emotional support and guide them in setting career path goals. By observing mentors, a teacher can learn teaching tactics that create fun and innovation in the classroom, but the role of a mentor goes beyond just demonstrating tips and tricks. A great mentor can change the trajectory of their mentee's career. They can be a part of their mentee's Professional Learning Network (more on this later).

Finding My Perfect Match

When I looked for my perfect match, I looked for a great teacher whose students excelled. That was extremely important to me. When I passed by my future mentor's room (Shirley Echols), I listened to how she taught, and I observed how she acted throughout the rest of the school building. I also paid attention to her performance at faculty meetings. At one faculty meeting, I learned that my future mentor's data exceeded state expectations—she didn't just look like a great teacher; she had results. I wanted my students' success to model her students' success.

I also had several conversations with my "perfect match" to determine if I could foster a relationship. I needed to see if she was approachable and supportive. It was a plus that she taught the same grade as me, as I could use her strategies, resources, and materials with my students.

Over the years, my mentor became my confidante and my emotional support system. When I had problems with administrators, students, or parents, I would go to her room for a pep talk so that I would be in a place to enter my room with confidence and the desire to persevere. With all the ups and downs of teaching, there were a few times I wanted to leave my building, but thanks in large part to my mentor, there was never a time when I wanted to leave the profession.

At the end of my first year of teaching, my students scored exceptionally well, even on the state assessment, due to my mentor's guidance. The data did not have to show me that I was doing an exceptional job because I could see my students' overall growth. The data was just a confirmation that I had survived my first year. My perfect match continued to support me through many more years of teaching, showing me what it means to be a teacher leader.

What Makes a Good Mentor?

To become teacher leaders, teachers need to understand how to find their perfect match. Teachers can look for their ideal mentor down the hall from their classroom or find someone in a different school. They can even find their perfect match on a social media outlet. As a teacher looks for their coach, it's essential that they look for someone who they want to emulate. Everyone needs someone who they can look up to and depend on.

There are many traits that make up a good mentor. Here are twelve traits that you should look for in your perfect match and develop as you strive to become a teacher leader.

Listens

Listening is a useful skillset to have as a mentor because there are times that the mentee will need someone to listen to them. When mentors listen, they can pay attention to what their mentee says. They offer useful feedback that will help the protégé make the best decision. The mentor can also challenge the protégé by providing solutions or asking probing questions of them.

Being a great listener helps the mentor empathize with their mentee because they learn from them through their conversations.

The mentor begins to be more compassionate, and a dedicated relationship can form between the two of them. They begin to understand how to communicate effectively with their protégé. They also know that, just as it is essential to listen to their protégé, they must permit the protégé to listen to them. It truly takes a collective effort.

Gives Feedback

Mentors understand the importance of providing their mentees with feedback. Feedback can be verbal or written and permits the protégé to grow inside and outside their classroom. When the protégé needs feedback from classroom observations, the mentor can watch the protégé and then develop a clear picture of what they need to say to them. The mentor can review lesson plans or help provide feedback over various initiatives implemented by the protégé. They know exactly what to say and how to say it.

Mentors want to uplift their mentees and want them to be successful. Great feedback leads to the mentee making changes for the benefit of their students and their career. A good mentor will offer continuous feedback and guidance. They also know the importance of following up with their feedback by checking in periodically. Regular feedback resolves issues that have developed and fosters confidence, motivation, and action.

Is a Role Model

A role model is someone you can look up to. People want to emulate them because they show others what success looks like. The protégé wants to be just like their mentor. They want to be just as successful as their role model or more!

The mentee admires the accomplishments and integrity of their mentor. The role model is loyal, and they have a desire to show others that they lead by respecting and collaborating with people. They understand the value of fostering a relationship and can often be seen discussing with others for the benefit of the students or the profession. Role models set high standards, so they challenge their peers and students alike.

A good mentor is also aware that people are monitoring them, and they work hard to do things right. They know that a negative issue or concern can change how their protégé looks at them. The role models invite their mentees into their classrooms to observe them. They model effective best practices so that the protégé can learn new strategies and methods.

Role models enjoy their role, and they want to create positive change within the educational systems. They are smart individuals, and they know how to navigate all sorts of situations. They are experts in several areas. They know their strengths and weaknesses and are not afraid to share who they are as individuals because they understand the importance of their role.

Celebrates

Mentors love to celebrate with and alongside their protégé. They serve as their coach, cheering them on. They understand the importance of celebrating accomplishments and want the protégé to know that they are proud of them. They know that words are powerful and can be used to uplift or tear down their protégé.

Their goal is to build up their mentee and encourage them to succeed. They use words to inspire, which makes their students and protégé want to do much more. They create ways for other people to celebrate their protégé inside and outside the school building. They want people to know that their protégé has been successful.

Is Committed to the Mentee

Great mentors are committed to their protégé. They understand the role that they need to play in their protégé's life. Often, mentors work with their mentees outside the classroom as well. They take time regularly to communicate with their mentee and do not need someone to advise them on when to meet or what type of support is required.

They know their protégé's strengths and weaknesses and they work with them to make sure that they can excel in their school community. They spend time with them on and off the clock to build a lasting relationship. They become familiar with their mentee as a teacher and as a person. It is vital for teacher leaders to know that their mentor is there for them throughout their career.

Shares Their Career Path

Mentors share their career path, so their protégé can figure out the direction they want to take as an educator. When the mentor shares their career path and goals, it gives the protégé insight into the various opportunities available to them. The mentor can share their wisdom on how to accomplish goals along the way. They can show their protégé how to do what they did so they can obtain their goals.

Mentors know the importance of offering guidance and strategic steps to their protégé. They help them develop a career path to follow. Teachers can have a great career if they know what they want to accomplish and how they want to—mentors get them on the path to the finish line by helping them establish a career plan.

Motivates

It is important to find someone who can motivate and encourage teachers in the profession. A motivator helps to drive teachers' excitement in the workplace. When teachers have a motivator, they have a desire to be committed to the work. A motivator can inspire teachers to stay in the profession while putting forth their best effort. In addition, a motivator helps to create a positive mood and keeps the teacher positive about excelling in and out of the classroom. When teachers find joy at their workplace, they can influence other peers in a positive way. A motivator also promotes a culture of belongingness, and they can truly change how teachers view their career.

Has Expertise in the Field

Being mentored by an expert in the field can play a significant role in a teacher's career. Experienced teachers are content area experts who can support other teachers in improving their craft. They are extremely knowledgeable about how to get students to accomplish desirable goals. They are accomplished in several areas of education. They work tirelessly to use their voices to advocate for students, teachers, and their school community. They bring a wealth of wisdom, and their knowledge can transform teachers. Finding the right expert can help with professional and personal growth.

Is a Network Developer

As teachers evolve into leaders, it is essential that they learn how to collaborate and connect with other educators and organizations. A mentor boosts teacher confidence by showing them how to foster a relationship with various stakeholders. They can help leaders understand what to say and how to say it. Mentors can also model how to communicate with others as well as give teachers opportunities to practice their communication skills. They encourage teachers to network in order to help advance their careers. The experience that comes from networking with other teachers and organizations opens many doors for teacher leader growth.

Is a Trainer

In the teaching profession, continuous learning is inevitable. A teacher needs a mentor who not only can train them to be a highly effective educator but is also willing to take on that role. Trainers offer support in and outside the classroom because they know that a teacher must extend themselves in many directions. They help with planning, designing, and creating authentic learning experiences for students because they simply want the best for them. Trainers are often hands on, and they enjoy modeling and demonstrating for their mentees. They want to share their expertise to promote growth. Finding a mentor who constantly wants to support you on your path to teacher leadership is not easy, but it is well worth it.

Is an Organizer

A mentor who is a great organizer can help you maintain your career in a healthy and balanced manner—adjectives not commonly used to describe the life of a teacher. Mentors model positive leadership traits since they know how to delegate responsibilities and guide others to be productive educators. They know how essential it is for teacher leaders to maintain control over their careers, so they maintain adequate, organized records for plans to run effectively. They are wonderful examples of planning ahead.

These mentors are ideal for keeping a teacher on track during especially busy or stressful times. They are goal- and detail-oriented and they make sure that they can accomplish their vision.

They also support teachers in setting and establishing goals. These mentors help teachers organize what they learn and make plans for incorporating new skills while maintaining old ones.

Is Respectful

Respect is fundamental to any human relationship. It is important to select a mentor who respects you as their protégé, and whom you respect. Aside from being necessary to hold the relationship together, a mentor who shows respect understands the importance of being an empathetic listener. They demonstrate purposeful listening skills. They listen to your concerns and desires, and they offer constructive feedback only as needed. They respect what you share with them, and they keep all shared information to themselves.

Respectful mentors do not mind acknowledging their protégé. They want others to know who they are assisting in the profession, so they can extend opportunities to the teachers that they support. In fact, they want others to highlight their protégé successes. They also find opportunities to praise others, since they know that they can strengthen relationships by doing so. They show kindness and respect to others. We all need mentors who cherish and respect us. When we find such a person, the friendship is likely to be everlasting.

As you evolve into a teacher leader, you will need to find many mentors for various situations and times. Once you learn the skill of locating your ideal mentors, you will be able to identify your perfect match in every phase of your career.

Mentorship Never Ends

How often do we resist asking for help when we need it? In the teaching profession—and life—trying to figure everything out yourself is hard; asking someone who has been where you want to make it infinitely easier.

I needed a mentor to survive my first few years in the teaching profession, but the need for mentors did not disappear after that. I have relied on several mentors throughout my entire teaching career to help me overcome obstacles and reach milestones in my career.

When I nominated for the Presidential Award, I sought out a mentor. I called on several awardees in my state to share their knowledge and tips on how to achieve my goal. One teacher informed me that the process was too difficult, and she did not feel that she could support anyone. Another teacher informed me that she was going to support another teacher. Of course, I was disappointed, but I was glad that those doors closed because that motivated me even more to accomplish my goal!

Sharla Steever did not hesitate in aiding me. She read my application and pushed my thinking with questions, offered resources, and provided suggestions. Instantly, she became my "Shero." I could not have survived without her. I went the extra mile in my learning experiences because of her. I did not want to fail.

When I submitted my application, I was confident that I had given my best effort. That following summer, I was contacted and informed that I was a finalist. Two years later, I was notified that I received the Presidential Award for 2008. I had so many emotions. I cried, laughed, and shouted because the odds were against me. Thank goodness, I accomplished my goal! I genuinely believe that everyone needs a mentor at almost every point in their career.

The Three Mentor Relationships Every Teacher Needs

Throughout my years of teaching, I have found that there are at least three types of mentor relationships that every teacher needs at all times in his or her career:

The Peer (Iron Sharpens Iron)
Peer mentors are vital to avoid burnout in the job. Many great teacher leaders seek peer relationships because they want to help grow other leaders by sharing their expertise, but they also want to keep current with best practices. Peer mentors genuinely

understand that the game of teaching is a give-and-take relation-ship. You must be willing to give, not just take.

Peer mentors are on the same level because they are in the same profession. They may be on different career levels, but they have the passion and the drive to do the work. One peer can serve as the mentor and the other can serve as the protégé. At other times, however, they can collaborate to offer support and guidance to each other regarding their work. The mentor can learn from the protégé and the protégé can learn from the mentor. One leader sharpens another leader until they accomplish their desired goals.

Peers can function as mentors for each other by sharing expertise and doing their best to make each other succeed in the profession. They can support each other's strengths and compensate for each other's weaknesses. A seasoned teacher can learn new and innovative ways from a colleague or novice teacher.

Teaching jobs have many challenges, and it is vital to have teachers who can collaborate on projects or planning to help with the workload. It is beneficial when two colleagues support each other because they can help shape the profession with their relationship. After all, two colleagues may share the same interests, vision, and goals.

The Judgment-Free Ally

Judgment-free allies are wonderful mentors to have as a teacher. They can come in the form of a colleague or friend, are someone that you can depend on, and you can use them to enhance your pedagogy knowledge. However, they're more than just a source of good ideas; a teacher enjoys the relationship they have with their judgment-free ally.

A judgment-free ally is someone who does not judge the leader. Instead, they serve as a confidante and a voice of reason. The teacher leaders go to them for advice and support. They can help relieve the teacher from the stress that comes with the job, and they can help teacher leaders forget about the problems that come with the profession.

They are someone you trust with critical issues. They do not judge, but they uplift teacher leaders, encouraging them not to give up. They also provide feedback on various projects and on the aspirational dreams of the teacher leader. They celebrate the teacher leader in making sure that they continue on a path of greatness.

Judgment-free allies are key to teacher leaders staying in the profession because they have developed mutual trust and respect. Building-level principals can also go to the judgment-free ally to help with communication with their teachers.

The Senior Mentor

A senior mentor is a person who is a veteran in the field and who possesses a unique talent and skill set. They are good at what they do, and other teachers admire their work from afar. They have a successful career full of accomplishments and service. They can share their career path so that teacher leaders can create their own vision and goals.

Because senior mentors understand the ins and outs of the professions, they can serve as valuable role models. Teacher leaders desire to emulate them because they want a similar career or some of their same accomplishments. Senior mentors are well-connected in the field, and they can help with recruiting, supporting, training, and giving advice. They can serve as a sounding board to potential teacher leaders and help teacher leaders with their career path opportunities.

Summary

It is vital to find mentors to help you matriculate throughout your career. Mentors will offer guidance and support to help you navigate your way to success inside and outside the classroom.

Stop and Reflect

- ◆ Why is it important to have a mentor?
- ◆ What type of mentor do you need right now? Why? How would it be beneficial?

5

Navigating Key Relationships in Your School and Community

Great teaching isn't about getting things done or compliance; it is about building great relationships with all stakeholders.

We've all seen teachers who work so hard to get their students to comply with rules that they entirely miss the opportunity to inspire their students. Your students need to see the human factor come out of you to encourage buy-in and build relationships. It is important to focus on relationships instead of compliance. This chapter is about avoiding that mistake and harnessing the power of positive relationships inside and outside the classroom.

Good Relationships Make You Better

When I first started teaching, I quickly realized that developing relationships with students, families, and teachers is essential in the teaching profession. It was essential that I connected with them to ensure my success as a classroom teacher; it is still essential in my career today. You know as well as I do that a teacher leader can't do much leading without positive relationships with others.

Although I sought to build relationships with students, families, and other teachers, one group with whom I did not try

DOI: 10.4324/9781003229537-7

to build relationships with the administrative team. In fact, I avoided the administrators.

Have you ever tried to avoid certain administrators at your school? Back then, I avoided the executive team as much as possible. I got along fine avoiding them for several years until I decided I wanted to advance in my career. For obvious reasons, I couldn't expect to do that by running away from the people making the big decisions.

Thinking about mingling with the administrators made me nervous. However, I forced myself to do it, and as our relationship began to develop, the chief administrator at my school encouraged me to explore my leadership options. I was grateful, and that led to me advancing in my career. I've long since overcome my fear of administrators and have seen over and over those relationships with administrators are just as important to the success of teachers as are their relationships with students, families, other teachers, and members of other organizations.

As my career advanced, I had opportunities to frequent unique spaces where I networked with various educational leaders. With each passing year, I set and achieved goals to meet new people and share my passion for teaching and my purpose as an educator. When I found colleagues who felt the same as I did, I shared some of my personal goals and dreams. I found that when I opened up to them, they would do the same, sharing their personal and professional goals with me too. Before such conversations would end, I shared my contact information with like-minded individuals, and we would stay in touch. I would run into some of them on consulting jobs or in fellowships. Having these relationships made it much more enjoyable to collaborate on classroom initiatives and opened many doors for me.

Relationships Are the Penguin Hole of Teacher Survival

Have you ever seen a penguin hole? Penguins often congregate around holes in the ice to fish for food and then return to the safety of the ice. For certain types of penguins, these holes are essential for survival.

In education, relationships are just as vital for teacher survival. Relationships matter to teacher leaders for so many reasons. Through building relationships, teacher leaders not only increase their career opportunities but also improve their social and emotional well-being. They continue to work on their communication skills so that they can communicate with individuals effectively. They learn how to express themselves to individuals who support their work vent to their support group. Their colleagues become not only partners but friends.

As you know, we all need someone to whom we can talk to when we face challenges and celebrate successes. Teacher leaders are no different because they have invested the time to create a web of positive relationships, teacher leaders know those to whom they can turn.

Teacher leaders understand they need certain critical relationships at different times in their careers. The relationships that are the most important in their career depend on the teacher leader's journey at a specific time. However, although they may not need something from a relationship at the time, teacher leaders diligently foster and maintain long-term relationships with all stakeholders because they know they cannot do the work in isolation. They also seek to make the world a better place and know that relationships give them influence.

Teacher leaders create relationships with students, teachers, educational leaders, parents, and organizations because they understand that these key players make up communities. To build a community, teacher leaders must be committed to knowing more about the people they work with. They understand that relationships are integral to the school system, and they are committed to connecting with others to forge ongoing committed relationships.

Finally, teacher leaders genuinely care about those with whom they associate and draw strength from the positive relationships in their lives to meet the challenges of their work. Authentic connections are critical! Without the proper relationships, teacher leaders cannot reach their potential inside or outside the classroom walls.

Key Relationships to Navigate

Teacher leaders need various relationships in different capacities, times, and for various reasons. They nurture their relationships with their bosses, peers, students, families, and community partners as they navigate through their careers. These relationships may run through a cycle of highs and lows or vary over time. Some of these relationships form based on specific challenges or goals. Among the most important relationships that a teacher can give his or her best effort to maintain, I have found the following relationships to be the most important.

Your Boss: Top-Down Support

Teacher leaders need to have a relationship with their bosses (administrators) because they will inevitably need administrative help in supporting local communities. Administrators understand community leaders because they have walked a similar path. Administrators are often able to see the bigger picture, and they share diverse perspectives with teacher leaders. They provide teacher leaders with critical feedback, and great administrators follow-up to make sure tasks are carried out.

I asked one of my colleagues and the 2017 Delaware Teacher of the Year, Wendy Turner, what she thought about the importance of relationships with administrators. Here is what she had to say:

> With educational leaders, it's important to form relationships at all levels if possible. Part of being able to do this well lies in our ability to understand and empathize with them in the context of their challenges. Without this empathy, people at different levels of the education system fail to understand what each teacher is going through in their part of the system. I have strong relationships with administrators, district office officials, those working at our state department of education, and local and state board members.

Your administrators can be a lifeline for you in your work because you can rely on them; you do not have to do it on your own. When doing something challenging, take time to converse with your administrators to ensure that they are doing the right things to help things run smoothly.

To illustrate this with a sports analogy, your bosses are the coaches, and you as a teacher leader are the quarterbacks. On the field, coaches and quarterbacks work together to create their perfect team and win games. Most administrators celebrate the success of their teachers' success and will not mind you being in the front. Exceptional bosses accept the "bottom-up" approach to leadership because they understand that teacher leaders make things happen for the school community.

Administrators are on your side; they have common goals such as students' achievement and social and emotional development. Not only will your bosses help you fulfill your role as a teacher leader better, but they will also provide you with opportunities to advance in your career and make your voice heard at district, state, and national levels as you take time off to share your passion for the profession and your message to others.

Your Peers: Creating Culture

In the words of Wendy Turner, "Connections with other teacher leaders are VITAL for teacher leaders. Often, teacher leaders exist in a vacuum at the classroom level where their leadership is either valued or perceived as threatening. Staying connected with other thought leaders around the country and around the world provides a community of like-minded individuals who know exactly what you are going through and who can be supportive."

Teacher leaders collaborate with their peers in the profession to ensure that students and their school community thrive educationally. Teacher leaders know that one person cannot create significant change on his or her own, but that dreams can come true with the right team.

As another associate of mine, Carlanda Miller (known as "The Magical Teacher"), put it, "It is important to have a relationship with other teachers because this is a very hard job. We need to lean on each other. We need each other to make it."

As you assemble teams of your own, seek dependable peers. The right people on the team make for more creative creations, more solutions, and better ideas. Work with your peers to plan for school activities, school improvements, and students' success. Discuss problems and trends that you see in your school communities. When you are overwhelmed, you will find that being surrounded by colleagues who are comfortable sharing with you and each other will calm you. Make professional and personal connections with these teachers. They will provide inspiration and courage to you. Additionally, over time, your influence as a teacher leader will inspire them and help them achieve their goals; they may become teacher leaders themselves. Being surrounded by other teacher leaders is the best place you can be for your own success and that of your school.

Students and Their Families: Holding Leaders Together

Teacher leaders want to earn the trust of students and their families because they know that everyone must work collectively to help students grow and reach their full potential. Teacher leaders want to provide students and families with comfort, encouragement, and motivation. Teacher leaders understand that students and families must have a vested interest in the education system for that system to be effective.

Parents and guardians are the children's experts when the children are home, and teachers are the children's experts when the children are at school. There must be a two-way relationship between parents and guardians and teachers. In the pursuit of educating the next generation, parents and guardians dig a tunnel from one end, and teachers dig a tunnel from the other end; both are working to get a breakthrough for the benefit of the children.

Stephen Ritz advises, "If you want to be credible, let me tell you something: start talking to grandmas. And I say that because in my community, I don't need the police to get things done; I've got grandmas, and hell knows no fury like a bunch of grandmas in the middle of South Bronx."

"We must connect authentically with families so they know that we are there for them and will work hard to secure positive outcomes for their children with great effort and perseverance," said Wendy Turner. "As part of my open house presentation,

I always share about my family life, activities I enjoy, and my strengths and weaknesses to let families not just listen to me but know me. It's critical to get to a place of connection so we can work together when challenges arise. We need to see, hear, and validate our families as much as our students. An authentic relationship is a necessary ingredient in the recipe for success."

While working with parents and guardians is critical, we cannot overlook the students themselves. Though young, students know a great deal about many issues, and you should ask for their opinions and value their perceptions. Teacher leaders often seek their students' input. And while you're asking them what they think, show your students that you care about them.

Stephens says, "Children who have access to one kind, caring adult in life, no matter where they live, will succeed in life. So be that kind teacher. Caring adults' kindness is the only thing that you can give away, and you get it back ten times in return. Now, it takes a little effort sometimes to be kind, but the accolades that I like, oh, he was so kind. He was so fair. I don't want to be that mean teacher. I don't want to be that grouchy teacher. I want to be the guy that when a kid needed a hug, I was there. That, to me, is the most important thing in the world that I believe in them."

Doing so creates tremendous benefit; when students know that their teacher cares about them, they meet and exceed expectations. All children work hard for a loving and caring teacher. If you want your kids to succeed, you need to be that teacher.

Carlanda Miller shared this with me about her experience building relationships with students:

> It's important to have that relationship because kids don't learn from people they don't like. This is very true. Kids also deserve respect, and they should be treated with respect. Just because the students I work with are little, doesn't mean that they don't have bad days, they don't have attitudes. You just need to teach them how to handle their big emotions. Relationships are really important with students.

By building loving relationships with your students, you can do immeasurable good in terms of students' social and emotional well-being. When appropriate, spend one-on-one time with them to create a personal connection with your students. Listen to their stories and implement future activities based on their needs and desires. Their narratives create the culture and climate of the classroom and school community.

As an example, during the pandemic, my second-grade students were at home with their families, and they saw the injustice manifest in the death of George Floyd. Consequently, my students were curious about the issues behind the issue, so I planned a few lessons to address race. I called these lessons "Superheroes Combat Racism." Students created superhero puppets and wrote a paper on the following topic, "If you were given a superpower to combat racism, what would it be and why?"

The Community: Leading Out

The school is the heart of the community. Stephen Ritz makes a valid point on why the community is essential to teacher leaders. "I'm not an accidental tourist. I live there. I work there. I walk those same streets. So, having credibility in my community is amazing. I say 'Hello' to every single person." Most people come to visit me in my community and in the communities, I work with, whether it's in the South Bronx or in Dubai."

Teacher leaders know that they are a part of their communities and they must tap into their community. Consequently, it is essential for teacher leaders to foster a relationship with community partners. Teacher leaders do this by inviting them into their classrooms and schools. Teacher leaders want community influencers to help shape the school landscape by offering their expertise to students and families. Teacher leaders share challenges being faced in their schools, giving community partners a chance to be part of the solution. Teacher leaders aren't afraid to solicit funds, resources, and advice from the community members because they understand their job to advocate for their students.

In response, community partners help schools fulfill their missions in the community. Indeed, community members depend on the schools to create future leaders. Therefore, community leaders need to be aware of what is happening in the schools and be invited to participate where they can.

As a teacher leader, you should invest in getting the community involved. Your school's administrative team can help you make that happen. Even if you encounter opposition in building relationships with community members, work hard at it. Those partnerships will help your school function in ways it never can on its own. With an example, my mother and I visited Little Rock Central High School National Park, the first high school to integrate in Little Rock, Arkansa. I asked the park ranger that would she zoom with my class and Micheal Dunlea's class, and she agreed to speak to the students. After the zoom call, I informed her that I would love for my class to visit and I asked about a grant for my class. My students were able to visit the historic site due to a funding source from the National Park.

Yourself: Knowing Your Limits

Decorated teacher leader Michael Dunlea responded to my questions about teacher-leader relationships in this way:

> "Teacher leaders gain when they engage with all stakeholders. If what we do impacts all of society, then all of society is where we must cultivate our relationships. We must know them, and they must know us. One often-undermentioned relationship is the one with yourself." Teacher leadership is a second career on top of a highly challenging day career of teaching. We must maintain a deep understanding of ourselves in knowing our physical and emotional limits in order to remain effective and important to our most critical stakeholders, our families and ourselves.

In a profession in which we give so much and so often of ourselves, our relationships with ourselves are too often overlooked. But it's just as important to have a good relationship with yourself as it is to have good relationships with your students. You have to really treat yourself well and take care of yourself if you want to survive—and thrive—in the education field.

The Motivating Power of Relationships

You will encounter many different stakeholders over your teaching career. Some interactions may make a lasting impression, while others will be short-lived. Teacher leaders are motivated to build lasting relationships whenever possible since they know that it takes many invested parties to advance education and increase student achievement. So, take time to create meaningful one-on-one relationships which expand beyond the scope of your teacher leadership; don't rush cultivating relationships with stakeholders.

If creating these relationships seems overwhelming, know that not all teachers start out knowing how to build relationships. I did not. Over time, you should seek training from organizations and mentors. But in the meantime, you may be asking what it takes to create relationships with key stakeholders. Here are a few key qualities I have found most helpful for fostering such relationships.

Be an Empathetic Listener

When you listen empathetically, you experience the world like you never have before. Excellent listeners observe others' passion for their work and are in a place to give and receive advice and support. Throughout my teaching career, I have had many opportunities to encourage teachers to pursue leadership opportunities based on our conversations. For instance, a colleague was curious about pursuing STEM endeavors. I encouraged her to apply for the NSTA-SHELL Urban Award. She received the award. Teacher leaders show their peers they are listening by encouraging worthwhile opportunities. Empathetic listeners also serve as a sounding board, which can provide helpful feedback to others.

Be a Confidant

A confidant is someone others can confide in. As a teacher leader, you should keep all details of confidential conversations in a closed vault. By doing so, others will know that they can depend on you. When an individual talks to a confidant, he or she takes a risk in being vulnerable. Vulnerability allows people to connect and have difficult conversations. You must create a safe space for others to share experiences if you hope to win their trust. You will also find friendships much easier to make.

Being a confidant isn't just about keeping secrets. It is about being someone that people can rely on. You want to develop partnerships with these people, and you want to demonstrate that they can trust you to have their back. They may want you to support their projects or events, assigning you a role to play. Being trustworthy with information will keep people from losing faith in your ability to contribute. Professionalism is an integral part of the profession. You must show that you are determined to learn, grow, and lead.

Be Approachable

You may find it hard to make friends if you're aloof, proud, or reserved. Instead, be approachable. You want people to see you as being open for collaboration and conversation. People view an approachable person as being available and easy to connect with. When you are approachable, you and those you get to know can learn from each other. In a team setting, you can create synergy.

"Being an educator is so incredibly hard and all consuming," Wendy Turner told me, "That we need our networks of support to not just survive but thrive. We are not a silo but part of a larger machine functioning for the good of students, families, and the community … The best way to form authentic relationships is to share our humanity and our vulnerability with each other."

Be a Storyteller

Sharing stories allows people to hear your passion and purpose for teaching. Stories grab people's hearts and capture their minds. No matter how far into your career you are, you have many stories in your tool kit. You should offer stories about your students, classes, and experiences in the community. Feel free to share stories from your personal life as well to help people get to know you.

When you tell stories, be careful not to turn conversations into pity parties. Remember to remain positive and focus on the things that can be changed. It can be powerful for others to hear of your challenges and successes, so be authentic. Those listening to the stories can envision your compassion for the students you serve. Being an optimistic storyteller can help change society as well as show the best version of yourself.

Be Patient

When working with others, it is essential to be patient. Patience is a skill and trait that develops over time. In meeting someone new, some teachers may not respond in the manner you wish. You may ask them to contact you, for example, and they may or may not. Relationships take time, and you must be willing to be patient. When initiating relationships with others in your field, consider providing them with the same "wait time" as you do students. If you do not hear back from them, you should reach out to them at some point. Educators are extremely busy, and sometimes you just need to revisit the conversation and resend your message. Usually, they reach back out after the second the same time around. Having patience is key! Accept that it is a part of every relationship.

Be Jovial

I remember once meeting a certain politician on Capitol Hill. Before meeting him, I researched him and found out what he liked, such as the Tennessee Vols football team. When I met him, we had a great time laughing about sports. His photographer captured that moment and posted the picture on his website.

A person cannot build a relationship with you if you are too rigid. Appropriate humor and a relaxed attitude go a long way to connecting with others. You can find joy in laughter and use it to make situations less tense and awkward. Having a sense of humor is also an act of generosity since you are sharing yourself with others when you laugh with them; you are allowing them to see your authentic self because what they see most of the time is just you as a serious worker.

Being an educator is hard work. Let down your guard and relax around other people. Laugher allows everyone to release anxiety. When you are happy and filled with joy, you can give up the need for control. This will help others relax and become comfortable sharing with you and even bond with you. However, it is essential to read your audience. Some people can function in rigid relationships and do not enjoy humor with colleagues, etc. When you meet those people, be respectful and don't let it get to you.

Martha Mcleod sent me the following:

> Stakeholders involved in the education of children—students, teachers, families, and educational leaders—all play key roles in the educational success of students. Therefore, I am constantly building rapport with as many stakeholders as possible including community members that can possibly help to enrich my outreach programs. All of these relationships are important to teacher leaders. We cannot excel in our careers without the many connections woven into our array of friendship and professional acquaintances.

As you work on building and maintaining strong relationships with students, families, administrators, community partners, and fellow educators, take every opportunity to create relationships with everyone. Anyone who impacts a child can help you move on your journey, even the bus driver, secretary, or building engineer. Many of these relationships will help your students and your school be the best they can be. Some of these relationships will advance your career. A few will become lasting and fulfilling friendships that keep you going throughout the years.

Summary

Building the right relationships is critical to keeping you and your students on a journey of constant improvement and self-discovery. When you establish an open-door policy and welcome relationships with participants in the school community of all types, it provides an extraordinary experience for building relationships. Your relationships will be fulfilling and key to your career advancement.

Stop and Reflect

- ◆ Which quality do you most need to work on from the "Motivating Power of Relationships" section? Which is mostly a strength of yours currently?
- ◆ Why are relationships important to teaching?

6

Building a Reputation of Positive Transformation

What do people think about your work when you're not around? That's your reputation and brand.

In the business world, people often talk about "branding" themselves, their company, or their message. Your brand extends beyond your presence and is defined by what people say behind your back, for lack of a better term. If you don't build your reputation, someone else will build it for you. In the teaching world, it is important to do something similar to brand building in the business world by building your reputation in the school community. Stakeholders visualize what teachers believe in and how they navigate in their classrooms. When you are intentional about the messages and results from those associated with you, people will begin to convey your strategies and methods to other stakeholders. This is a powerful way to make an impact, stand out in your network, advance your career, and gain the support of stakeholders.

I did not learn the importance of building the right reputation until later on in my career. As it turns out, teacher leaders know the power of reputation and consciously create their own.

In 2006, I pursued National Board Certification. I did not make it the first time, but I was not surprised because I struggled in science integrated with math. Some people might have given

DOI: 10.4324/9781003229537-8

up and not tried again. As a former athlete and the daughter of a football coach, I have perseverance in my DNA.

To accomplish the National Board Certification, I had to grow professionally in STEM. I recall calling several educational STEM organizations and asking them how to convince students to ask questions and, through self-discovery, find the answers. I stayed at the school until 10:30 p.m. nightly to research and plan.

Through the process, I fell in love with STEM, and my students did too. STEM. Right before my very eyes, I watched my students change how they felt about STEM. The results were remarkable!

My students keep coming back, years later, to tell me about their STEM careers. My hopes and dreams for my students became a reality. Years later, I was recognized for being a Cool Science Teacher in Scholastic. When word got out about my success, educators and organizations wanted to learn more about my STEM innovation strategies and methods. I became known as the teacher who creates worthwhile STEM opportunities for the underserved and underrepresented population. I became known as the teacher who saw inspiration in white lab coats for her second-grade babies. Without trying, I built a reputation for myself.

What are you passionate about?
What makes you happy?
What do you want to do for students and yourself?

These are a few questions that you can ask yourself to help you discover your passion, which is one of the most important parts of building a reputation; you don't want to be known for something you aren't passionate about. Passion projects unlock teachers' potential inside and outside of the classroom walls. These projects enable them to create experiences that both they and their students enjoy.

Student success is the center of the bullseye as far as teacher leaders' aims are concerned, and ultimately, students are what drives teachers to be passionate about their work. But students aside, there are many ways to bring excitement into your classroom. For example, you may want to blog or go on an international trip to learn more about schools in another country. Whatever you do, the magic happens because you are doing what you love to do. People notice individuals who shine a light on their passion.

Passion projects help teachers like you be creative, productive, fulfilled, and mindful. When you engage in them, you will naturally see yourself creating change since you are following your dreams. I encourage you to think about what you enjoy and start thinking about what changes you want to make for your students and yourself.

Another way to craft your reputation is to seek professional learning experiences that help you become an expert in your field. Many professional learning experiences can help to nurture your passion. You take the initiative in deciding which learning experiences will be most beneficial to you. Passion projects and professional learning experiences help teacher to discover what they value.

Where the Magic Happens

Magic is often associated with magic tricks or magicians. Magic is spectacular and awesome to see. Personally, I love seeing illusions happen right in front of me. It makes me excited, and I want to see more magic happen because I cannot believe it. Whenever I see a magic show, I'm not the only one who leans over in her seat and grabs her face in excitement.

This level of magic needs to happen in the classroom. Students must find joy and excitement in every lesson. They should enter ready and eager to learn. I believe that before a teacher can graduate to the level of teacher leader, he or she must learn to create magic in the classroom for all students. True teacher leaders shine brightest in their classrooms. To be one, you must create magic in your classroom. You know your magic is successful when your students are excited to learn and discover new ideas. The root of this magic—and the impact and reputation that come from it—is your passion.

Teacher leaders use their passion to implement various strategies, methods, and techniques for teaching their students. Because they love what they do, these teachers' magic gets better and better. Innovation in the classroom is driven by wanting to connect students to what they want to learn so they can fall in love with learning.

Teacher leaders use their classrooms as the center stage for creating those magical experiences. Stephen Ritz reminds us, "So whether you are a ballet dancer, a computer scientist, or an incredible chef, bring those talents to your classroom because children are inherently curious, someone that they want to know. And if children want to know you and they want to work with you, therein lies the pathway for success. Don't keep patting yourself on the back. Just be you, baby. Be you. Absolutely."

I love Stephen's energy as he reminds us to be our authentic selves. Just be you, teach and create magical moments for your students and you!

Teacher leaders create stories in the classrooms, and their students experience many magical moments. This magic branches out to all valuable stakeholders. Stakeholders see the results and want to know more about the teacher leader's work. But before this magic can spread, it must happen for the students in your classroom, so create a space where students are happy and engaged!

Now, let's look at some strategies for how to create magic in the classroom and build your reputation as an extraordinary teacher leader.

Develop Your "Why"

Teacher leaders identify their purpose in leadership and develop a game plan. They understand that students should come first. They love their students and school communities. They often think about their students' communities and the challenges that their students are facing. Helping their students overcome these challenges becomes their "why," and keeps teacher leaders up at night. It is an endless flame that keeps burning until teacher leaders resolve the problems that they can, and until their students are better off.

Understanding your "why" is not only motivating but also helps you develop a strategic plan to address the challenges you are passionate about. It makes it easy to find purpose and meaning in your work. There is nothing quite like the desire to create everlasting change inside and outside the walls of your classroom.

Once you find your "why," you may feel overwhelmed by the endless problems in the world that you want to solve. Just tackle one challenge at a time.

And when it comes to helping your students, remember that student agency is vital to their progress; you can't change students or their situations if they don't want you to. Listen to students' and families' stories to connect with them to address their needs. Show that you care about their ideas by implementing them and encouraging them to take action to encourage and motivate their school community. Get everyone involved in creating change. Doing so is a complex task, but if you stay focused on your "why," you will find a way.

So, take the time to learn your "why" and watch it create wonderful teacher leadership experiences and opportunities for you! When developing your why, you can ask yourself, what content knowledge do I enjoy teaching and what pedagogical approach do I enjoy implementing. I develop my "why" by thinking about my students' identity. As I see it, it is essential that I know who my students are as individuals, what they have access to, and what they don't have access to. I also think about my identity, and as a minority teacher, I share a lot of things in common with my minority students. I address issues that impact my students academically, emotionally, physically, and socially. Also, I expose them to personal experiences in my life—or things I have not experienced but know—that can help them in their lives. My students inspire me to develop my why. I think about what they are missing in their lives, and I plan and implement accordingly. I also enjoy teaching STEM to my students and enjoy focusing on inquiry-based learning as my pedagogical approach to teaching.

Form and Maintain High Standards

Teacher leaders have high expectations for themselves as well as for their students. They have high standards to ensure that students can thrive and achieve in America. They raise the bar high because they know that the bar is at least that high in other parts of the world. Teacher leaders want to afford their students the same (or better) opportunities for success in life as do those obtaining education elsewhere. They share their expectations with all stakeholders to make sure everyone understands his or her role.

Students learn more under high expectations. These expectations can apply to in-class activities, not just test scores. Knowing this, I give my students achievable but challenging tasks in class. For example, I once had my students create an animal out of Styrofoam that attracts or holds birdseed after they learned how birds help to disperse seeds. I had them use lab sheets while engaging in the engineering design process.

Simply having high standards is not enough. Stakeholders should be aware of your expectations so they can also support students in living up to them. You should also hold yourself to high standards in terms of the lessons you teach. The curriculum you are given serves as a blueprint for creating lesson plans, but it is only a tool and a means to an end. Your high standards may lead you to implement other resources and materials to create rigorous experiences. Your higher standards will help you address equity as well to ensure that all students advance. Use your high standards to create academic challenges and growth for your students and to motivate you to touch each of them. Do not settle for less. Failure to reach students is a failure for any teacher.

Stick with a Theme

Many effective elementary teachers feature themes in their classrooms so they can capture students' attention. They select themes that students love and can relate to. They use these themes to physically create an environment that is inviting to students. Teacher leaders love creating the right classroom environments for students.

Also, they find opportunities to think outside the box to inspire the next generation of future leaders. Often, they focus on a concentrated content area that they love. Their excitement and passion shines through and it inspires their students to achieve at a higher level.

For instance, I love teaching STEM, and my students wear lab coats during inquiry-based learning. My focus is on getting students to enjoy STEM. Wearing lab coats is a simple thing, but my students find joy and hope in those jackets. I devote valuable time and effort to making STEM topics come alive in my classroom.

Use themes to create experiences in your classes and to grab and hold on to your students' curiosity. There's no one way to do this, but it does require creativity and some work. As you continue to build your reputation, choose one area in which to become an expert in order to change students lives. As you effectively use thematic teaching, your reputation will grow as stakeholders recognize you for the unique themes that you have created for students. For example, I have become known for addressing inequities for students of color in STEM. It is my goal for them to see STEM professionals that look like them.

I challenge you to think about a concept or content area that you want to teach really well. It may take some time to create a masterpiece of a learning experience, but it will be a remarkable sight when you finish!

Be Okay Wearing Many Hats

Although having a personal brand is important, don't let it confine you to one activity. You will have to wear many hats to enact the change that your students need.

Policies from state departments, districts, and your school drive many of the experiences your students have at school. Such policies dictate how the classroom functions. As a teacher leader, you may need to make your voice heard to lobby for policies that affect your students. In some battles, you may need to lead far away from your classroom at the district, state, and national levels. You will need to stay current with changes that occur, so you can be an advocate for your students and their needs.

As you have already realized, you must also wear many hats in your daily teaching activities. You must research and prepare content; you must lead a classroom; you must be diplomatic with parents and other stakeholders; you must motivate students who are struggling; you must maintain data and records; you must actively communicate with all stakeholders; you must lead activities or programs; you must oversee the dropping off and picking up students; and the list goes on. Of course, you serve in these many capacities because of the love you have for the profession and for your students.

Some teacher leaders like to implement several themes or projects in their classrooms because they want to keep current. Doing so requires wearing multiple teaching hats. I love to address STEM, global learning, and civil education in my classroom. It takes a lot of planning to ensure that I implement these various topics. However, these topics are essential for the students I teach. Roles, policies, concepts, and curriculums change quickly in education, so be prepared to adapt so you can do what is best for you and your students. As you do so, you will create magic and others will see it.

Share Your Message

Sharing your message allows others to make personal connections with you and buy into your vision. Your message is a powerful part of the reputation you have as a teacher. As you share your message, listen to the messages of others. You will learn much that will help you in your teaching career.

One place to share your message (by talking about your passion and the change you are trying to bring about) is on social media. When you put yourself out there on social media, people will be able to easily learn more about and connect with you personally and professionally. You can also post about your best practices and student successes.

In addition to social media, you can create a reputation for yourself by sharing your stories on blog posts, websites, panels, and at conferences. Stories are powerful and moving to stakeholders. When teachers share tactfully, they empower other educators to share their stories, and everyone is better off.

Carlanda Miller (the magical teacher) shared the following success story of sharing her message on social media.

> I think that sharing your message on social media is bene-ficial. There are people that aren't even teachers that follow me and tell me that they feel uplifted by seeing my posts and the positivity. I've talked to people from different countries and different states that tell me that they enjoy my posts, or that they tried something I suggested and thank me for the idea.

I think I've been viral maybe about four times, which led me getting on to *The Kelly Clarkson* show three times. The first time I was a guest, but it was a surprise guest. She zoomed me in and shared my video from my classroom.

And then, the second time, I was zoomed in again, she wanted to show my virtual classroom because my virtual class-room looked just like my actual classroom (it has a castle and everything). And so, she showed me my classroom and talked to me about how it was teaching during COVID.

And the third time, it was for teacher appreciation. I was there live. I didn't get to talk to Kelly, but I was in the audi-ence, and she gave us $5,000 for library books and some other stuff.

In sharing your message, use whatever platform works best for you. The important thing is that you share it!

Note: Always be positive on social media and ask parents, schools, and districts before posting about your students and work on social media. Remember to protect your social media footprint by being positive and motivating.

Summary

In education, teacher leaders create a reputation for them-selves based on their passion and the change they are trying to make in the world. Innovating in the classroom and having high expectations for yourself and your students is a major part of this. Your brand is the lightning, and your reputation is the thunder. Both create a magnificent sound and a beautiful sight for the world to view and are powerful forces to be reckoned with.

Stop and Reflect

- ◆ What is your pedagogical approach to teaching?
- ◆ What are you passionate about implementing in a class or school community? Why?
- ◆ What would you like the teaching profession to know you for?

7

Growing into Teacher Leadership

Success doesn't mean anything without continual growth and development.

As teachers, we know that certain character traits and mindsets are essential for high performance; we see the power of mentality on learning, development, and achievement every day in the lives of our students. To realize our full potential, teacher leaders must develop character traits and mindsets of growth. We must be open-minded. We must be willing to work on ourselves. We must be eager to learn and experience new things.

In short, we must be everything that we hope our students are. By leading by example, we will not only inspire our students but also become more effective teachers and efficient administrators ourselves.

Over my decades of teaching, I've identified twelve crucial aspects of perspective and character that educators must develop if they hope to grow into teacher leaders.

Be Dependable

People look to leaders to make their lives easier. If you can't be depended on, you can't lead; that's just a fact of leadership. Being dependable means that you do what you say you're going to do.

To understand how critical, it is to be dependable, just think about those whom you depend on. For example, in my current

DOI: 10.4324/9781003229537-9

role, I depend on several individuals to help me with planning school activities. I also frequently rely on a new teacher, Ms. Bryson, to assist me. She and I often collaborate after school to complete tasks such as applying for grants and hosting STEM Fest (a program at our school). She is always available and reliable. It is a great feeling to know that I have someone to depend on.

As a dependable teacher leader, you should be able to answer yes to the following questions:

- Do I submit and complete tasks in a timely fashion?
- Do I follow through on all assignments and projects?
- If given an assignment or task, do I meet all the requirements with precision?

Be a Risk-Taker

As the saying goes, "Growth doesn't happen in your comfort zone, and comfort doesn't happen in your growth zone." Taking risks is uncomfortable, but for exactly that reason, it leads to growth. Our students take risks when they guess at an answer in class, sign up for honors or AP courses, try new extracurricular activities, compete for student body presidency, and so on. While these risks may not seem very risky to us adults, they are important learning opportunities for students.

Teachers also need to take risks; if we avoid risks to stay in our comfort zones, miss personal growth and impact in our schools and communities. Here are a few beneficial ways you as a teacher leader can learn to take risks:

- Face your fear of trying new things: inside or outside the classroom, pay attention to things that scare you; when you find something that does, face your fear and do it.
- Don't worry about failing. Remember, you only fail if you never try (or quit trying before you reach your goal).
- Create innovation *outside* the classroom for the benefit of the students. Here is an example of what this might

look like: Several years ago, I hosted a Carnival Physics event for the community. At the event, stakeholders learned about physics using carnival rides. Several people believed it could not be done, but I showed them my plan and convinced them to buy into the vision. I collaborated with fellow educators, a church, and business organizations to bring Carnival Physics to life. It was a risky undertaking because it was new and innovative, but the endeavor turned out to be a success.

◆ Solicit funds and grants for the school community.
◆ Give 110%. Stretching yourself to give more in everyday situations will increase your capacity to take risks that require your time and energy and increase your chances of success in risky endeavors at the same time.

Have Integrity

By "have integrity," I don't just mean being dependable (though that's obviously important too). The aspect of integrity I'm talking about here has less to do with effectiveness and more to do with honesty, confidentiality, and commitment to upholding ethical standards and organizational policies.

Oh, the most important one, honesty. You got to say what you mean and mean what you say. I'm not really impressed. I've met some of the smartest people in the world, literally. I've met some of the wealthiest people in the world, literally. At the end of the day, what impresses me most is honesty and integrity that you say what you mean, and you mean what you say. You show up daily and do the work, and that's something that everyone can do. Listen, not everyone is born with a silver spoon, but everyone can be honest.

I agree with Stephen Ritz that everyone can have integrity. There are thousands of instances in which a teacher leader should have integrity. Here are a handful:

- Do things (big and small) with fidelity. If someone tells you something in private, keep it confidential while looking out for his/her best interest.
- Be loyal to your school's standards and administration.
- Be honest with all stakeholders.
- Trust other people.
- Listen to your moral compass.
- Play by rules and follow policies and procedures.

Have Grit

No teacher ever said their job is easy. Teaching is one of the most difficult jobs out there. Some days, pushing through the daily challenges of being a teacher—the long days, the politics, the rambunctious or dramatic students—requires true grit.

We teach because we want to help our students find success in their lives. We need to have the mental fortitude to push through our own challenges if we expect our students to learn to push through theirs. Here are some suggestions for increasing your grit inside and outside the classroom:

- Don't give up on tasks and goals, no matter how small. As I once heard, "how you do anything is how you do everything."
- Determine to succeed in whatever you do. Don't set a goal or accept a responsibility to which you aren't committed.
- Set an example that challenges others to succeed.
- Advocate for your students. It is imperative that you speak up for students by sharing your voice at the table; students need us to share their stories.
- Hold on to a long-term vision of where you want to be and who you want your students to become.

Part of having grit is having the patience to keep moving forward when things aren't going your way. When asked about the critical traits of teacher leaders, my colleague and fellow teacher

Wendy Turner, who is a wonderful example of a teacher leader herself, put it this way.

> Teacher leaders should have an abundance of patience. Patience for students and new colleagues when helping them to find their place on a team. A sense of humor makes a job a lot more enjoyable, too.

Another aspect of grit is flexibility. Carlanda Miller (The Magical Teacher) named flexibility as an essential trait of teacher leaders.

> "… every day is an adventure," she told me. "Every day is going to be different. You have to be able to move and groove and adapt and to change; it's going to be something different every day. Nothing is going to run the same. You may get lucky and get your class rolling … But you will never know what's going to happen when you get in there."

Be a Team Player

No school can be run solo. Educating students and creating a school environment of growth need to be seen as the team efforts. A teacher leader can't effectively lead as a teacher if he/she is competing against other teachers or working in isolation. Teacher leaders need to lead, and that means being a team player. Ask yourself these questions to assess how you can improve in the team-player aspect of being a teacher leader:

- ◆ Is working together as a team with other teachers and administrators important to me?
- ◆ Do I fall into the trap of silo working?
- ◆ Do I think I can do a great job without a team?
- ◆ Do I have the right players on my team? If not, do I know how to get them on my team?

- Do I play in the role I was assigned, or do I take over other people's roles?
- Do I play for the collective win or to be better than my coworkers?
- Do I cheer on other members of my team and encourage and motivate them?

Sergio De Alba, 2020 National History Teacher of the Year, told me the following about being a team player.

> One characteristic a teacher leader should have is to see what every stakeholder can bring and focus on elevating their contribution. If you are focused on what you bring and what brings you attention, you tend to lose the desire of stakeholders to become involved. Whenever a recognition is made, I always share the success with the efforts of all stakeholders. The reality is that when a program you have initiated is successful it is due to the efforts of many. Stakeholders continue to want to work towards a goal when they can see that the leadership acknowledges and appreciates their efforts.

Be a Designer

Teacher leaders are creative, and they know how to give their creativity structure. They don't just produce ideas, they design projects, curricula, goals, and initiatives. Creativity without structure is hard to apply. Structure without creativity is about as useful as reinventing the wheel.

- Get passionate about designing worthwhile projects; where there's a will, there's a way.
- Think outside the box when planning by encouraging ideas that are "out there."
- Take time to enjoy a creative project and take it to completion.

- ◆ Focus your planning on the needs of students and other key stakeholders.
- ◆ Scaffold your ideas into an organized structure.
- ◆ Practice thinking deeply and set aside space to dream up new and innovative things.

One way I've found to be a designer is in bridging racial gaps. Discussions about race are now taking place in every corner of American life—in boardrooms, in City Halls, and on the streets. Since George Floyd's death in Minnesota, I have felt a new urgency to get kids talking about racial realities. I know talking about race can be very difficult for younger children, but it is important for us to have the conversation because if racism is going to end, that end must start with our students.

I take my students on field trips to see places where historic battles for school integration played out. To put a bright shining light on racism, I had my students to wear sunglasses while we discussed race. I had my students talk to Zaid from South Africa about how art heals people, and he shared a puppet with the students. The students followed his advice and created super-hero puppets that combat racism.

Fieldtrips, interviews, and puppets are creative methods of accomplishing the initiative of fighting racism. Combining structure and creativity is exactly the balance designers need to strike.

Be a Reflective Practitioner

Everyone knows that being a problem solver is important for success in most endeavors. Being a reflective practitioner takes that a step further by following up on solutions and adjusting as needed. As an illustration, sometimes teachers must adjust to units or lessons after they have been taught. These teacher leaders think about what went well and what did not go well for individual students. They then adjust accordingly. This conscious adaptation helps teachers move forward for the benefit of students. After you create a program, pay close attention to the implementation to see if it's having the desired effect.

Key traits of reflective practitioners are as follows:

- ♦ They see problems and desire to develop solutions for others.
- ♦ They evaluate the strengths and weaknesses of their solutions with data.
- ♦ After implementing each solution, they measure the outcome and reflect on the results.
- ♦ They adjust their solutions as needed, striving for continuous improvement.
- ♦ They have a worldwide view; they find ways to improve by analyzing the world at large.
- ♦ They are lifelong learners who want to grow and get better.
- ♦ They want to push limits and reach new milestones.
- ♦ They do what is best for students and think about how they can expose them to appropriate content or topics.

Be Confident

I know from personal experience that it is easy to feel like a failure as a teacher. Sometimes you feel like you're working long and hard but not having an impact. Other times you second guess yourself and your abilities. Teacher leaders move beyond these feelings and know that they can and *do* change lives. Here are some tips I've found helpful for being confident:

- ♦ Believe in yourself.
- ♦ Know your impact: think about the impact you can have on your students and their families.
- ♦ Put deliberate time into crafting your content.
- ♦ Practice delivering your content to a variety of audiences.

Teacher leader Michael Dunlea—who, among other awards, has received the Presidential Award of Excellence in Mathematics and Science Teaching in 2018 and is pursuing a second master's degree in teacher leadership—suggests that we "have courage, without it you will fail. There are forces out there that will push back with great energy, and it takes straight up courage to challenge the status quo."

Similarly, Wendy Turner believes that confidence is a primary characteristic that teacher leaders should possess. "Teacher leaders should possess a strong belief in themselves for when they come up against challenges," she says. "In addition, staying grounded in a 'students first' mindset will be an asset that guides their actions which is hard for others to argue with."

Think Analytically

Teachers often have an intuitive sense of what to do and say in the classroom and while working with stakeholders. Teacher leaders back up and refine their intuition with data. They are skilled at gathering and interpreting data that show them how to refine their craft, change more lives, and advance in the profession. The following are examples of practices teacher leaders employ as they think analytically:

- ◆ They seek feedback (data) on their teaching and the progress of their students.
- ◆ They observe their own practice in depth.
- ◆ They welcome feedback and look at it objectively.
- ◆ They interpret the data, then adapt according to what it tells them.
- ◆ They react quickly to the observations of their data.
- ◆ They recognize general trends in teaching and student progress at the school and elsewhere and convey these trends to others.

Nurture a Competitive Spirit

Although too much competition among members can negatively affect a team, competition can help teams bond together and individuals excel. For me, the core of useful competition is striving to be the best you can be and never giving up in that pursuit.

Do you have a competitive spirit? You may think you know the answer to that question already but asking yourself the following questions will help you see ways in which you may need to guide and nurture your competitive side.

- ◆ Do you not want to lose because you want to win, or because you don't want to fail?
- ◆ Do you play to win?
- ◆ Do you have confidence in yourself?
- ◆ Do you want to be on the right team?
- ◆ Do you love to celebrate successes, both large and small?
- ◆ Do you persevere through adversity, fueled by a vision of a perfect outcome?
- ◆ Do you cheer stakeholders on because you understand it is imperative to make people feel special?

In 2007, I wanted to apply for the Presidential Award. I remember calling on a few people to assist me as my mentors. One educator I came across turned me down and stated that she would instead help someone else. She believed that the teacher she favored over me would be selected as the Tennessee finalist and win for our state.

I was shocked by her rejection, but I am glad that she said what she said! Many people would have given up at that point and questioned their self-worth. Instead, I stayed up late at the school and conducted research on how to implement inquiry-based learning with elementary students. Also, I used what I learned from National Board Professional Standards in the area of science integrated with math. I was determined to prove this educator wrong, and I worked hard to submit a worthy application. In 2008, both I and the mentee of the educator who had rejected me were both finalists, but I was selected as the Tennessee finalist and represented our state in Washington, DC. As a former athlete, I certainly have a competitive spirit, and it has served me well in my career; my goal is to play to win for my students!

Be Flexible

As mentioned in the grit section, teacher leaders must be flexible. In education, there are frequently new rules and mandates, and you may have to change or adapt your practice to accommodate policies. Each year, you will receive a new group of students and families. You must learn about the students and families, since no students in your class are ever the same. You must plan accordingly to meet the needs of the students and families. Not only that, but as a teacher leader, you may need to assist your colleagues at a moment's notice, or the administration may have some requests for you. When COVID-19 happened, every teacher had to be flexible and adapt how they taught students. Teachers had to persevere to continue teaching students in a different way (remotely or in a hybrid model). Here are a few tips to help with being flexible.

- ◆ Look forward to adapting if changes are being made.
- ◆ Be willing to ask questions.
- ◆ Be willing to navigate change.
- ◆ Stay positive.
- ◆ Talk to a colleague to share your concerns.

Be Empathetic

Empathy is the ability to lead others while understanding who they are as individuals. When teachers make decisions, it is beneficial to consider the feelings of those affected by the decisions. You make decisions with those consequences in mind. Their stories should be important to you and may cause you to shift your paradigm on some issues. Here are a few questions to ask yourself to ensure that you are being empathetic.

- ◆ Do I have interest in their lives?
- ◆ Do I understand what they are saying to me?
- ◆ Do I adjust from their stories?
- ◆ Do I need to ask clarifying questions?

Developing each of these twelve attributes on your path to becoming a teacher leader won't happen easily or overnight. But striving to do so will increase your success and fulfillment as an educator inside and outside the classrooms.

Summary

Teachers become teacher leaders by developing the character traits and adopting the mindsets typical of teacher leadership. Among these include having an open mind, persevering through adversity, nurturing integrity, and so on. Though not easy to obtain, these attributes are the foundation of leadership and positive impact inside and outside the classroom.

Stop and Reflect

♦ Which characteristics stood out to you in this chapter and why?
♦ Which trait would you most like to develop and why?
♦ What trait would you add to this list and why?

8

Why Reinventing Yourself Will Elevate Your Career to New Heights

Life will always require us to keep evolving.

As a teacher, I reinvent myself every year. Each reinvention results in a new and improved version of me best suited to the challenges in my classroom and personal life.

Why do I reinvent myself? I do it for the benefit of my students. Things are always changing in our world, and my students enter my classroom each year being exposed to new situations and ideas in their home lives. I want each student to have the best outcome possible and know that I need to adapt my teaching to motivate and encourage my students in the fast-changing circumstances of our society. Reinventing myself and my teaching is a prerequisite for taking my life and my teaching to the next level.

A few years ago, I was teaching social justice to my students. It was a fulfilling and enjoyable topic for me to teach. I decided that my teaching habits needed to be reinvented, so I broke up classroom exercises with field trips.

While we were learning in class about some of the greatest steps to social justice in modern America, I took my students to locations where they took place. We went to Little Rock Central

DOI: 10.4324/9781003229537-10

High in Little Rock, Arkansas, which is the first high school to be racially integrated. We visited the Civil Rights Museum in Memphis, Tennessee.

This is a simple example of reinventing myself for the benefit of my students. I wanted my students to be inspired to be current leaders in their own small way, not just future leaders someday, and I figured the best way to do that would be to connect them with current events in tangible ways. I knew my students could benefit from me doing something above and beyond the norm, so I did just that.

You must master the art of reinventing yourself if you are to have a maximum positive impact on your students. Teacher leaders regularly reinvent themselves for the sake of their students. I have the privilege to associate with some powerful teacher leaders who know the power of doing just that, and I asked a few of them two simple questions:

- ♦ Why is it important for teacher leaders to continue to reinvent themselves?
- ♦ How do you continue to reinvent yourself?

Their comments illustrate what reinventing oneself in the classroom can look like.

Majorie Brown

Why: "As society and economies transform, teachers need to keep up with change and be a part of preparing children for change—whether the change is in technology, politics, careers etc. Then teachers also grow and see other possibilities, and this may lead to options of career change, which may still benefit the education sector. Still more reinventing is needed when a teacher reaches retirement age, which I am on the cusp of. I need to look at post retirement options to reinvent myself and still be able to share my skills, play a meaningful role."

How: "I hope to mentor new teachers. I have worked in literacy issues for over 15 years—I hope to continue this, as the need is so great in my country. However, combining my passion for children's books and literacy is also a possibility—for example, in the Climate Action project my pupils and I did worksheets on climate action for under-resourced inner-city projects, using children's books on climate action, so two issues were combined there. Maybe I will be part of writing historical fiction on lesser-known women in my country! This can still be used to build literacy and feminism. At the same time, as social change happens, issues of importance change—from racism to climate change—and therefore listening and reading, keeping up with the debates of the day is important to make informed choices. Teachers need to be lifelong learners."

Martha Mcleod

Why: "The world is ever changing, and as teachers, we continually morph our skills to meet the needs of the children in our classes. Everyone eventually finds themselves in a rut. By challenging ourselves to delve into a new creative project with kids, we learn alongside them and our own excitement for the profession."

How: "I continue to reinvent myself by dabbling in creative projects with kids that I initially have little experience in. An example of this would be the birding program I launched. In the beginning, I had several members of an ornithological organization teaching me along with my students. Over time, I honed my skills and can now run the programs."

Sergio De Alba

Why: "The needs of our students are ever changing. My program is modified annually to best suit the needs of the students in each class. By continuing to focus on what is needed by students, I provide a more relevant program, which in turn achieves greater success. Additionally, when you continue to grow as an educator, modify your approach, and then see increased success, it makes the process more enjoyable for both student and teacher."

How: "Never stop learning and keeping an open mind to new approaches. I take every opportunity to develop and improve with workshops, professional development sessions, and conferences. I also focus on having as many new experiences as possible because they assist me in developing new approaches and programs that can be taken back to the classroom. I have begun to travel a lot more with a focus on developing lessons on the experiences in these trips. Having photos and personal connections to what you are teaching comes out as you are speaking, and students can feel this excitement. The excitement breeds engagement and the idea that experiences are more than things that just happen to you. Experiences are opportunities to connect new knowledge to your own life and from there create new ideas, connections, and innovations."

Wendy Turner

Why: "Teaching is an art not a science, and as our students and their needs continue to evolve and change, especially now, it's critical that we evolve to meet their needs. I am about to start my 12th year in the classroom, and so much has changed since I started teaching. My core values and principles have not changed, but how they work in action certainly has. I reinvent myself for my students, those I serve. They don't deserve a teacher who doesn't evolve. Stagnation gets us nowhere."

How: "I continue to reinvent myself by being a lifelong learner. I pursue training on topics I am interested in and challenge myself to know more so I can do better. I share vulnerability when I need assistance and remember that I don't have all the answers. The blend of humility and the hunger to learn and grow serve me well in this area."

Michael Dunlea

Why: "We are lifelong learners and need to model for all around us, especially our students and other teachers, that learning and changing is never a finish-line sport. We possess gifts, talents, and skills that have yet to be discovered. The journey brings forward passions we did not know we held."

How: "I always keep my eyes open for the next opportunity to meet other educators and stakeholders who will challenge me and stretch my comfort zone. Over the course of many years, I have gone from struggling with a skill like public speaking to excelling and enjoying it. I also know that I have a lot to learn around equity. As a white male with privilege, I have been on a journey of learning and understanding the perspectives and experiences of people of color. It is important for me to grow in this way as an individual but also as an educator, so I can better meet the needs of all my students."

Claudine James

Why: "As a teacher leader, I am committed to seeking and finding more opportunities for student community engagement within the community. This is important in order to help me grow as a professional and be able to lead other teachers into doing the same."

How: "My first step is to create my annual PGP (professional growth plan). This is required every year before school starts. PGP outlines my yearly goals which not only reflect how I will enhance instruction and continue to grow as an educator, but it will also reflect my goals as a teacher leader."

Stephen Ritz

Why: "I think it's not about I haven't reinvented myself. I've been very receptive to change. And I think that's the important thing. People think of education as the sacred institution. I don't like the word institution. I think of Penal institution, medical institution. I don't like institutions. I like organisms. I like things that evolve. I think it's most important to be receptive to change, know who you are and then be receptive to change in the world. The best way to plan for the future is to be a part of it.

So, inventing yourself and being receptive to new ways of the world is really important. When I started teaching, there was no Internet. There were no cell phones. None of the things that are the critical tools that we use today were there then, but I was always receptive to trying to learn about them and incorporating them into my life."

How: "I continue to reinvent myself by being open to feedback. I love feedback. I'm on the recursive cycle of self-improvement. There is only one person in my family who always is right. That's my wife. I'm never right. I'm just determined to get it right. I think that if you realize your limitations as a human being, therein lies the opportunity to get layer on layers of support and opportunity that make you a better human being. I surround myself with people who I love, who I adore, who has something to offer. Then I multiply that by being around children as much as I can because they're receptive to all of it."

Michael Pope

Why: "Leadership is about reflection and continuously improving the educational experience for our colleagues, our students, and our profession. When a teacher leader invests in themselves through the reinventing process, they are becoming transformative and a living example to their students that learning is indeed a lifelong pursuit. The teacher leader who takes the initiative to reinvent and improve themselves is making a personal commitment to improve the profession and to position themselves to be ready to guide the next generation of learners toward success. It all begins with self-awareness through reflection that leads to reinventing based on best practices."

How: "I start with daily reflection and re-evaluation of my interpersonal and professional interactions. A lot can be learned by just taking a moment to reflect on the day, triumphs and obstacles and having a one year, three year and five year personal and professional growth plan. Curiosity is also how I reinvent myself. I keep myself learning personally and professionally.

I invest in myself by staying current in my field through professional development and conferences even when it is at my own expense. Also, I travel and learn languages to open my mind to global perspectives and other cultures. It's all about investing in yourself and put a value on education as a necessity of life."

New Day, New Students, New You

As expressed by these teachers, reinventing yourself is not something that should happen just once or twice. It is important to reinvent yourself on a regular basis to keep growing and meeting the needs of your students.

The core reason that reinventing ourselves as teachers is so critical is that the world is ever changing. As the world changes, the needs of students change. True principles and facts are constant, so in that sense, your material won't change over time. How you present that material and the person presenting that material (you), however, do need to change. You need to be different. You need to be up to date and relevant. You need to be on the hunt for new teaching strategies and methods. You simply cannot afford to be the same teacher today that you were ten years ago, five years ago, or even last year.

Although reinventing yourself will help your students, it will also benefit you personally in significant ways. For one, reinventing yourself leads you to fall in love with the profession all over again. This will bring joy back into your daily work. Along those lines, reinventing yourself will also help you avoid checking out or burning out; the constant adaptation will sustain you throughout the years and keep your career (and life) interesting.

Here are a few ways of reinventing oneself as a teacher that I have noticed to be effective over the years. Pick and choose the suggestions that resonate most with you or think up some other way to keep yourself and your material the "latest and greatest." The important thing is that you don't stay stagnant; today is the perfect day to reinvent yourself!

Keep It Fresh

Sergio nailed this point when he shared how he takes every opportunity to attend workshops, conferences, and professional development sessions, and how he focuses on "having as many new experiences as possible." The instructional events hone his teaching skills and expose him to successful practices employed by other teachers. The new experiences spark his creativity and passion for life. All of this together keeps his teaching fresh and exciting, and his students motivated.

It's important to live an exciting life because that excitement will bleed through into your teaching, and your students will be inspired by your passion for what you're teaching. Even if you aren't in love with the particular lesson or curriculum, you can still find ways to get invested in the topic and explore its relevance. Doing so is the best thing you can do to help students answer the age-old question, "When will I ever use this in real life?" In fact, they may not ever ask that question in the first place because what you are teaching is real in your life.

If you're wondering what you can do to keep your teaching fresh, one suggestion is to experiment with the latest technology and find ways to incorporate it into your classroom lectures. Whereas you may be used to route lecture and discussion, integrating technology may help you connect with the new generation of students are both tech-savvy and do not like to sit still. Technology has a certain "wow" factor that keeps students entertained (at least for a while) if used effectively.

Another suggestion is to modify the structure and routine of your class period. Most changes, even if structural, can enhance learning and retention by increasing novelty. Teachers can periodically adjust the agenda to provide students with a new routine. They can also establish a theme each day to excite students.

For instance, Monday could be "Monday multi-culture" read-alouds, where students take turns listening about various cultures aloud. Tuesday could be "Take it to the text Tuesday," where students read an article and cite text-based evidence.

Wednesday could be "Writing Wednesday," where students work on their writing skills. Thursday could be "Technology Thursday," and students could engage in blending learning using technology to research and explore. Friday could be "Fun with STEM Friday," when students learn about STEM topics. Mixing things up can add excitement to any classroom.

Be a Lifelong Learner

Wendy Turner is a phenomenal example of lifelong learning. In her words, students "don't deserve a teacher who doesn't evolve. Stagnation gets us nowhere." By challenging herself to learn, Wendy is continually becoming better able to serve the kids in her classroom.

Lifelong learning need not apply only to classroom skills and techniques, although improving in that arena is always a good idea. As teacher leaders, we can be lifelong learners by learning about the subjects we teach, subjects we don't teach, or even topics that aren't covered in school. Being a lifelong learner is not so much about what you learn as it is about the commitment to always be expanding your mind. As the common saying goes, "If you're not growing, you're dying."

Carlanda Miller (The Magical Teacher) revealed this to me about her secret to lifelong learning:

> You can never know everything. I'm magical, but I don't know everything, right? I'm constantly trying to read, organize something or try something a different way or thinking about how a lesson went and trying to take a different way the next day. It's really important to never stop learning to be a lifelong learner because there's so much out there. I'm constantly trying to learn new things and try new things. Teaching is very hard, but you must be willing to do the work, and you have to be willing to own up when you don't know … It is just important to try to learn as much as you can because there's always going to be something to learn.

Stay Current with Research

Research informs teacher leaders of new discoveries and proven approaches in their field. Staying up to date with the latest research is important for keeping your teachings skills sharp and your subject knowledge fresh and accurate. A few great ways to keep up on the latest research are as follows:

- Attend webinars and online conferences with speakers in the educational industry.
- Connect with organizations that keep current with today's strategies.
- Pay attention to what is going on in society and look up related research.
- Ask other teachers and administrators what interesting research they've come across recently.

Another side of staying current with research is using research in the classroom. While it's important for you to be aware of scientific breakthroughs, your students may be inspired if you expose them to the cutting edge of research. In my class, for example, we skype with scientists and other STEM professionals. These professionals give my students exposure to their careers and the excitement of developing new technology.

Be Reflective

Teacher leaders are reflective by critically examining their progress and making changes accordingly. Consequently, reflection is what helps teacher leaders evolve to meet the needs of their students and advance in their careers. It starts with asking a variety of questions, including the following:

- Am I doing what is best for my students?
- Am I getting through to them?
- How can I build the stamina of my students?

- How can I continue to build their knowledge of current events?
- Am I addressing students' needs?
- How can I better address their needs?
- How can I more fully inspire my students to excel inside and outside the classroom?

Once you've asked yourself those questions and thought about the answers, be willing and intentional about change. The best intentions can't have an impact without action.

Over the years, I've seen a simple formula proven time and time again that should guide teacher leaders as they reflect on how they're doing. It looks like this:

Passion + Purpose = Student Success

Teacher leaders keep their passion ignited. They also ignite the passion for learning in their students.

Teacher leaders align themselves with their purpose by reflecting on their philosophy of teaching. They also help students find a reason to learn.

What is your philosophy of teaching? Is it different than it was a few years ago? If so, how did it change? Your philosophy as a teacher leader is likely to evolve with time. Never stay married to one iteration of your philosophy or teaching practices. Instead, link your philosophy to your "why" and let it adapt as needed depending on the needs of students. Your teaching philosophy is about the "what" and the "how." Those should always come second to "why."

As you practice being reflective, focus on your passion and purpose, and the passion and purpose of your students. When passion and purpose come together, success happens in the lives of students.

Go Outside Yourself

We all tend to stick to what we know—particularly if we make a living by being an expert (teacher) of a subject. Venturing outside of our comfortable realm of knowledge and experiences will inevitably mean growth for us personally. If we take the lessons and experiences we acquire back into our classrooms, we'll have an effect on our students as well.

One thing that can help with creating positive change is to get into the habit of taking on new perspectives. We can help students follow our example through something as simple as encouraging discussion in the classroom or pairing students up with new partners. These interactions can mold and shape who our students are and how they learn.

I've learned firsthand the importance of going out of my comfort zone. As a teacher, that's the only way to immerse yourself in new ideas and practices! Feeling uncomfortable is good because it means you're doing something different.

One area in which I had to leave my comfort zone was public speaking. I used to get nervous when faced with speaking in front of a crowd. When I was in America Achieves (a fellowship), they would sometimes ask me to speak to large audiences. I had to step outside myself to complete those tasks. It was never an easy feat, but I made myself give those speeches and they turned out to be successful. Today, I'm better because of those experiences.

On another occasion, I received several emails asking me to complete a video promoting higher standards in education. I ignored the email for several days because I was not comfortable with being recorded. Finally, I accepted the request. During the interview, a lady asked me a ton of questions, which I did my best to answer. I thought that I did a horrible job until I received an email from her telling me that I was outstanding. She even invited me to an exclusive conference in Orlando, FL and gave me tickets for nine others. That following summer, I attended the conference with the nine other educators whom I invited.

The beauty of going outside yourself is that it can change your life, and you alone can choose it.

It is a choice to reinvent yourself and take control of your life. In a very real sense, it puts your hands on the steering wheel of your life, giving you greater power to take your life and your students where you want them to be.

Embrace Discomfort

As I discussed in the previous section, the greatest learning happens when you are working outside of your comfort zone in unfamiliar territory. But it's not enough to simply leave our comfort zone; being outside of our comfort zone is uncomfortable, so if we don't have a tolerance for discomfort, we'll never stay out of our comfort zone long enough to learn anything. That's why we need to train ourselves to embrace discomfort.

I like the analogy of learning to ride a bike everyone gets injured when riding a bike. But a few falls, scrapes, and bruises are no reason to stop trying to learn. In fact, if you're not willing to go through that discomfort, you'll never experience the thrill of successfully riding a bike. Instead, you must continue to ride until you feel comfortable. When you can embrace discomfort for long enough that the situation becomes comfortable, then you know you've grown.

Teacher leaders embrace discomfort to grow personally, to become more effective instructors, and to set an example for their students. Embracing discomfort enables teacher leaders to take risks and to experiment showing up for their students in new and better ways.

Grow Your Network

Michael Dunlea said it right when he remarked that one of the secrets to his success is always keeping his eyes open for opportunities to meet other educators and stakeholders who will challenge him to grow. Networking can sometimes give you career advancement opportunities, but it almost always makes you a better teacher.

Teacher leaders take full advantage of the support offered by their colleagues and actively seek to grow that support system. Teacher leaders know that networking can lead to brainstorming, new strategies and techniques, inspiring stories, and helping with projects inside and outside the classroom.

Although the foregoing suggestions are not an exclusive list of ways to adapt to continually evolve to better serve the needs of our students, reinventing oneself is a key element of teacher leadership. How frequently and thoroughly you choose to reinvent yourself as a teacher will largely determine the speed of your growth and that of your students.

Summary

Teacher leadership requires us to regularly reinvent ourselves as teachers. Reinventing yourself brings joy and excitement into our own lives and inspires our students to engage with our material. As we reinvent ourselves through lifelong learning, staying current with research, being reflective, going outside ourselves, embracing discomfort, and growing our network, we will grow in our career and impact on the lives of the kids we teach.

Stop and Reflect

- ♦ How do you reinvent yourself?
- ♦ Which featured teacher's statement resonated with you? Why?

PART 3
Evolving as a Teacher Leader

9

Dare to Dream

You can only achieve success if you refuse to give up on your dreams.

Have you ever dreamed an impossible dream?

I have done that several times in my teaching career. I have set many worthwhile and audacious goals, but I was not sure if I would accomplish them or not. I accomplished some of these goals, but many times I would end up shooting for the moon and landing among the stars. My success as a teacher leader ultimately came because I never gave up.

In 2013, I was nominated for Tennessee Teacher of the Year, and I wanted to achieve that goal. During the spring of 2014, my principal notified me that I was in the running for the award. I was so elated, but I knew that I had to create an award-winning packet to advance as a regional finalist. Have you ever been nervous because you thought something was out of your reach? If you have, then you know how I felt. One of the reasons I was nervous was because I did not see any minority teachers as past winners of Tennessee Teacher of the Year. However, I was going to prepare and give it my all!

I reached out to a fellowship coordinator to provide me with constructive feedback. In the summer of 2013, while in Brazil at a global fellowship learning experience with the NEA Foundation, I discovered by email that I was one of the nine Core Regional Finalists! Of course, I screamed and cried because I had advanced!!

DOI: 10.4324/9781003229537-12

I formed a committee of educators and policymakers to support me. They prepared me for my interview by asking me critical questions and informing me about current policies. I also created a brochure to showcase my class and my work for presentation to the review panel. During my interview, I smiled as big as I could so they would not be able to tell that I was nervous.

After a few months passed, I headed to the banquet in Nashville. My family and friends came to support me. As my name was called for West Tennessee Teacher of the Year, my mom held my hand, and she said, "You got this, Melissa." I had my acceptance speech in my other hand, ready to share stories about my class and school community. Then they named the Middle and East Tennessee Teachers of the Year. We were down to three teachers. My heart dropped when they called another teacher Tennessee Teacher of the Year. Having made it that far was no small feat, but my heart was set on winning the award. That night, I remembered crying on my aunt's shoulders because I had worked so hard. I had accomplished other goals. Why was this goal so hard to reach? As she talked to me, she reminded me of dreams and informed me that there would be more dreams to chase. My love for my students allowed me to stop shedding tears, get back up, and dream a little more for them, for me.

I share this story with you to encourage you to develop your hopes and dreams. Like Nelson Mandela stated, you are a winner when you never give up. As teacher leaders, how can we hope to inspire our students to dare to dream without doing so ourselves?

Don't worry about what you do not achieve if you don't reach your audacious goal (or at least not in the timeframe you expected); that doesn't mean that you've failed. The fact that you fought to reach a plan that was temporarily out of reach means that you stretched yourself, achieved more than you would have with a more comfortable goal, and grew your ability to dream and succeed in the process. That's the beauty of shooting for the moon: even if you don't reach it, you still land among the stars, which is so much grander than aiming for a metaphorical mountain top and reaching it.

What kind of dreams should you develop in your teaching career? Although pursuing any personal hope or dream will make you a more inspiring teacher and mentor, your leadership in the classroom will be most effective when you specifically nurture aspirations of student success.

The dream of changing the lives of students is the reason most of us became teachers anyway. Though you may enjoy acclaim and career advancement when your students crush standardized tests, this dream is compelling when it isn't about you. Dreaming on behalf of someone else is a selfless endeavor ultimately rooted in love. This motivation exalts our initiatives and goals and gives us the strength to accomplish the impossible. In my experience, dreaming of the success of our students for their own sake is the greatest dream a teacher can have. Remembering that dream, setting audacious goals in line with that dream, and relentlessly pursuing those goals will fan the flame of your teaching success like bellows.

As you strive to improve, focus on your students, and watch your dreams come true. Dreams are good! When you fall short of your dreams, remember that the process is the reward. Grow and learn as a person through each "failure." Keep dreaming. When you accomplish one dream, find another. And if you consistently achieve your goals on the first or second attempt, *dream bigger!*

Stretch yourself to aim high and reach for more. When it comes to dreams, the greatest risk is the one you never take.

Play to Win and Strive for Excellence

Dreams don't come true unless you work for them. Although this means that reaching your aspirations as a teacher leader (and helping your students reach theirs) requires effort, there is another beautiful side to the equation: effort can make your dreams happen. *Your dreams are in your control.*

With our excuses essentially stripped away, we as teacher leaders need to wake up to the fact that we set goals to accomplish them, not just jump through the hoops of managerial encouragement. For this reason, we need to play to win. We must play to win for ourselves, our schools, and—most importantly—our students. We must commit to fulfilling our dreams with our time, reputation, energy, and heart.

Playing to win means striving for excellence with everything we have. Of course, we won't reach all our ambitious goals the first time around, nor should we. But striving for true excellence requires giving our best (more sometimes) and never giving up.

Playing to win does not mean that we allow ourselves to become crippled by perfectionism. We strive for perfection, but we don't require it of ourselves or our students. Doing so can be destructive and counterproductive.

Well-known author Brene Brown says, "Perfectionism is a self-destructive and addictive belief system that fuels this primary thought: If I look perfect, and do everything perfectly, I can avoid or minimize the painful feelings of shame, judgment, and blame."

People often fall into the trap of trying to be perfect—myself included. Some struggle more than others, but we're all affected by the temptation to tear ourselves down when we do our best but fall short of the ideal. Perfectionism is unforgiving, haunting us with past shortcomings (imagined or real) and future hypotheticals. It is also relative: no matter how much we achieve, we always see ways we could have done more or been better. Our efforts seem perpetually insufficient.

In short, being a perfectionist causes us to work out of fear—fear of not being good enough—and insecurity. Think back to the times you were consumed by perfectionist thoughts: did you feel confident in yourself? On the contrary, I suspect you tended to be on edge, doubtful, and eager to avoid criticism.

Perfectionism compels us to be perfect *now*. There's nothing wrong with striving for perfection, but a healthy mentality provides space for making mistakes along the way; those mistakes are indeed a large part of the growth process. We *cannot* perfect ourselves in any substantial way nor achieve an audacious goal without temporary failures along the way. Perfectionism convinces us that we cannot afford to make mistakes—now or ever. Consequently, it drives us to stick to what we're good at and avoid situations that push us out of our comfort zone.

It's hard to believe and dream—and hard to teach effectively—in a cage of self-imposed perfection complexes. Instead, do your best to root out perfectionism in your life. Don't expect perfection of yourself, and certainly don't expect it from your students. Strive for progress and expect growth. By going so, goals and dreams will be realized faster than you may expect.

Pursuing excellence (but not expecting perfection) naturally leads us into unfamiliar territory where our students and us can grow. Teacher leaders take risks for their students' benefit and their own. Mistakes can happen, and teacher leaders acknowledge their errors and forgive themselves. They reflect on their practice and make needed adjustments. They don't intend to fall short of their goals, but when they do, they dust themselves off, remember their dream, and learn to be better.

Setting Your Sights on Success

As teacher leaders work toward achievements in their educational career, their priority should be to focus on doing an excellent job for their students, the school community, the profession at large, and themselves. When aiming for success, here are a few tips to consider:

Be a Visionary
Teacher leaders maintain a higher vision and go after their dreams. This vision drives them to work to achieve their dreams, taking big and small steps to bring their vision into reality. They know that unleashing their creative side elevates their aspirations and fuels them with positivity.

Know Your Strengths and Weaknesses
Teacher leaders know who they are as educators, and they proactively take time to evaluate their progress, successes, and areas for improvement. Teacher leaders embrace who they are today as individuals and get clear on who they want to be. They

understand that it is essential to evaluate themselves. Along with assessing themselves, teacher leaders critique their work and character by observing their strengths and weaknesses.

Teacher leaders depend on their strengths to make an impact in the classroom and the education field generally. Their strengths help teachers successfully implement practices they are passionate about and compensate for areas of weaknesses. Teacher leaders are not blind to—nor paralyzed by—their weaknesses, and they work to overcome those weaknesses.

As an example, from my life, I love to try new things, but I find using technology can be complicated at times. But there is so much that you can do with it. To overcome this weakness of mine, I collaborate with colleagues who are technology gurus and get them to teach me and assist with projects. Teacher leaders seek out opportunities to work with others who can help compensate for their weaknesses and help them learn. As another example, suppose a teacher leader discovers that they have a disadvantage in teaching a particular concept. In that case, they will reach out to and collaborate with others who are more knowledgeable in that area or more comfortable presenting the material. Identifying your strengths and weaknesses is essential to long-term success in the classroom.

Embrace Your Authentic Self

As a teacher leader, you should embrace who you are as an individual. You should love yourself and live in alignment with your values and beliefs. You should not be afraid to discuss who you are, your life experiences, and what you bring to the classroom. Your students come to school to be taught by you (among others), not to hear material presented by a robot. The more of yourself you put into your teaching, the more your students will connect with you.

Yes, this means you need to bring your identity and experiences to the classroom; however, it is just as important to embrace your students' identities and personalities. When you do this, you can change the dynamics of what you bring to the classroom. Students need to see how teachers let go of being themselves. Teachers can also bring their personal experiences from their childhood or things that they wished that they were exposed to as a child. As we give of ourselves, it is crucial not to stagnate by only presenting students information that reflects our beliefs and values. We have to be willing to open doors up to our students.

Embracing your authentic self will also bring your dream to life. It's hard to dream without being yourself. That's why it is important to dream to make your dreams come true.

Embracing your authentic self also entails unapologetically doing what you believe to be best for your students. As a teacher leader, you shouldn't be worried about what other people think when you know you're doing what is best for your students and the profession. Rather than fretting over potential judgment from others, teacher leaders shine their light everywhere and capture their students' attention by sharing their authentic selves.

Your authentic self may change from time to time, and that is okay. As you learn and grow, your values and beliefs will naturally be refined and may even change. Never be afraid to be the real you today because of who you were yesterday. Be open to the process of discovery, growth, and change.

Stephen continues to inspire me when he says, "You need to embrace your superpower. Whatever your superpower is. That's how you become a teacher leader. My superpower is relationships. The funny thing is people think I'm a good farmer. I'm not a good farmer. I kill way more plants than I grow. I only take pictures of the living ones. But what I do is I inspire people to grow themselves, and that's really what it's all about for me."

Forgive Yourself for Making Mistakes

Mistakes are but successes written in pencil. Mistakes can be erased and rewritten until teacher leaders reach their accomplishments. Teacher leaders do not let the dark clouds of doubt, frustration, and regret linger over them. When those clouds do linger, teacher leaders recognize them as a clear sign that they are not in a good headspace.

No one is perfect. Forgive yourself for mistakes and start over again. Mistakes are to be learned from. Failure is only temporary. Teacher leaders know that failure is only a sign of incompleteness;

for them, the battle is not over until they win. Your success is just right around the corner. Let it go and move on.

Stay Humble

Only immature dreams are based on a desire to pull others down, even your "competitors." Mature dreams have a positive impact on others. As you remember the reasons you chose the teaching profession in the first place, you'll reconnect with a version of your dream that motivates you to succeed while helping others do the same.

When teacher leaders view their dreams in that way, they are staying humble. Pride drives us to be better at the expense of others, while humility inspires us to be better with others. Humility will increase your impact in the classroom and your relationships with your colleagues and stakeholders.

Commitment to excellence and the accompanying accomplishments can sometimes cause us to appear stuck up or threatening to others. Stephen Ritz says, "I'm a believer in giving credit to the people who hate me the most because if you give them credit and you're doing something good, they can't come out and be against you. Teachers always want credit. Give the credit and get the work done." While some people may always be offended by our successes, we can share them in a way that inspires others rather than makes them feel insecure. The key is to be positive and encourage others to pursue their dreams as well.

On the other hand, don't be afraid to mention the successes you are having. Invite others to share their accomplishments as well. A rising tide lifts all boats; you can be that rising tide to others and lift them when you are successful. Sharing the vision you are striving for can also be impactful. I have witnessed many times when a dream shared has boosted teacher morale. So be positive as you share your successes and encourage others to achieve their dreams too!

Celebrate All Victories

I will never forget that day I discovered that I accomplished National Board Certification. My principal did not want me to check my email that morning at school because that previous year, I did not accomplish National Board and I was devastated. I did as she suggested, but I had my teacher assistant check it. I remembered the words "Congratulations" written on the screen; I did not read anything else. I ran out my door, fell to my knees, shouting, and crying. My principal discovered me in the hallway and said, "I told you not to check your email." I told her that I did not check my email. My teacher assistant checked it. She laughed and held me for a while. That day, I celebrated becoming a National Board-Certified Teacher. It was a huge accomplishment for me!

All victories—big and small—are worthy of celebration. Take every opportunity to celebrate your victories; doing so will help with your mental well-being. No teacher ever said that their work is easy. Everybody celebrates the gold medals of their career, but those don't happen very often. Finding frequent, even daily, opportunities to celebrate small successes (particularly those that came through much effort) is tactic teacher leaders use to stay motivated and positive.

Contribute to the Larger Community

No teacher can do his or her work in a vacuum. Others help us in our schools and the community at large. While focusing on our students should be our priority, we teachers have a profound opportunity to do good in and lift our communities.

You're undoubtedly busy enough meeting your responsibilities as a teacher. Still, I've found that carving out time to work outside the classroom can benefit one's career and further one's teaching dream. Your contributions will elevate both the larger community and also your personal life. When you have the opportunity, it's always better to give.

Develop a Team

Every dream needs a support team. I don't know of any teacher who can complete his/her imagination in a bubble. You will need support from others along your journey, and others will need support from you.

Teacher leaders associate with a team that inspires and supports them. Some days, they gain ideas and new experiences from their group and are refreshed by the company of complementary personalities and worldviews. Some days, teacher leaders are comforted by commiseration with empathetic friends. Other days, they are challenged by mentors to dream bigger and do better.

Develop a Strategic and Sustainable Plan

Strategic planning is vital in clarifying where teacher leaders would like to go and how they will get there. Teacher leaders harness the power of planning to make their wildest dreams possible. They have mastered the process of creating strategic plans and use this skill often. They frame their vision with milestones and goals to motivate them and enable them to gather the resources and support they need. Strategic and sustainable plans are the directions that point teacher leaders toward their dreams.

One critical aspect of creating strategic and sustainable plans is sharing those plans with others. Sometimes we go down a rabbit hole to scheme up a brilliant strategy only to discover later that we overlooked simple issues or solutions. Others can test our plans for feasibility. Don't be the only gatekeeper to approving the plan to accomplish your dream. Your dream (and your future) deserves the best, so get feedback.

Remember Your Students

There is a danger in dreaming up grand goals as a teacher; the danger is that you may forget your students in the process. Remember that the heart of your dream should be a desire to serve your students. The well-being of your students is your first and foremost responsibility, and no certifications or recognition in your field can make up for failure to touch individual lives through your teaching. Put your students first, and other successes will follow.

Summary

Some teachers get worn down over the years. Others become more driven and inspired with each year that goes by. The difference is in those who dare to dream. While keeping their students at the forefront of their aspirations, teacher leaders stretch their limits, accomplish the unlikely, and set a positive example for students by harnessing the power of their dreams.

Stop and Reflect

- ◆ What dreams do you have for yourself, your students, or the profession?
- ◆ When was a time that you reached for the moon and landed among the stars?

10

Moments That Transform Teachers' Lives and Careers

Leaders are skilled at teaching others and take every opportunity to do so.

The life of a teacher is a lot like hiking a mountain. With every step you take, you draw closer to achieving your goal of climbing to the highest point. As you walk, your breath is taken away by how beautiful nature can be. You prepared for this moment to ensure that you were in the best physical, mental, emotional, and spiritual shape. Fatigue sets in on you, but you don't give up. You begin to build your stamina as you approach your destination. When you get to the top of the mountain, you celebrate that moment because you have accomplished your goal, and you are ready for the next adventure. The entire experience leaves you stronger, wiser, and more fulfilled. Though the hike wasn't easy, it transformed you.

The teaching profession is full of experiences that transform teachers much like mountains transform hikers. These life-changing experiences are what prepare teacher leaders to make groundbreaking changes in the educational world.

The form these transformational experiences take varies between different stages of your life and career. Some may happen because of situations that arise, and others may come from your planning—such as goals that you set. Your career may

DOI: 10.4324/9781003229537-13

also be transformed by following through epiphanies, innovation, or the ideas of fellow educators.

Sergio De Alba shared with me what transformed his career the most. He said, "In education, there are many opportunities to lead in the field. I have had the opportunity to participate in fellowships, certification programs, and conferences that have provided transformative professional growth. My approach is centered on experiences being the catalyst for developing improved education systems, making choosing one difficult. Instead, I would state that allowing an open mind and the input of the community I serve to create my approach has been the most transformative approach to creating my teaching methodology."

Like Sergio pointed out, participating in teaching-related organizations can provide you with many transformational experiences in the form of training, networking, and leading. Some even give you a voice at the table so you can fully engage. I have always felt appreciated and valued by such teacher fellowships and associations and am confident that, once you enter these spaces, you will gain much from what you are exposed to there.

Because each teacher leader is different, it's up to them individually where they should go next on their journey. Some transformational changes can come from failure, rejection, or success. When I asked Stephen Ritz what the most transformational opportunity he ever experienced as a teacher leader was, he stated that it was being fired. "Being fired because it makes you reinvent yourself," he said. "You could sit there and say, 'Poor me, poor me, poor me.' Or, 'This isn't fair.' Or you could do something great. Listen, the day they put me in the rubber room, that morning, I was on Good Morning America. I got a new job, so I don't see a crisis. I saw an opportunity. The doors were meant to close for a reason and open up the availability of new pathways of success. So my most important transformational professional opportunity is being fired because it didn't define me. It didn't end me. It just made me that much more resilient and that much more determined."

Some of the most transformational experiences in my career have been in moments when I was in a place where my voice and practice mattered. In each of these moments, I took my students with me on my journey because they indeed are my inspiration.

On one job (a project for Educators Rising), I showed a video that permitted my students to showcase who they were as a class community and who I was as a teacher. When the project was over, I had my students sing a song sharing what I told them about the project. Who is better to share your narrative than your students?

I have also been transformed by the support I have received from people and organizations. I am grateful for every opportunity I have received from them. It was the organizations and people that believed in me as a teacher leader that provided me with a space to feel empowered. When I felt empowered, I wanted to do more for all my students, and I felt encouraged to stay in the profession.

Teacher leadership does bring about opportunities for you to advance your career, but, most importantly, brings about change for your students. As Stephen told me, "The greatest reward that I get is seeing my children succeed. And that's the most important thing. The focus should not be on a reward or nomination because others will notice when you do the work. Trust me, the recognition and opportunities will come if you focus on your students."

There are so many educational experiences for educators that I was unaware of when I was young in my teaching career. The rest of this chapter discusses a few opportunities you should be aware of.

Advocating for the Profession

My first leadership opportunities came from the union. I learned how to advocate for the profession because of the association's professional community. They trained me on how to lobby for education. Early in my career, I served on committees and boards at the local and state levels.

The union also taught me how to communicate effectively with educators and provide learning experiences to enhance my teaching craft. One worthwhile learning experience was training on how to navigate the National Board process. The union extended opportunities for me to travel to lobbying events, teacher leadership trainings, and conferences.

The union provides chances for you to lead, learn, and grow at the local, state, and national levels. When you join the union, you can serve on committees or boards to support the profession. Also, you can be nominated for awards such as California Casualty and apply for grants or a global fellowship funded by the National Education Association (NEA) Foundation. The NEA Foundation is an excellent organization that supports educators and students. They also offer support for your classroom.

To sum up, the union is very beneficial, not just for advocating for you at the district, state, and national level, but also for providing you with opportunities to lead, learn, and grow as an educator.

Pursuing National Board Certification

My experience with the National Board was a time for self-development, reflection, and fine-tuning of my practice by completing a portfolio to demonstrate that I knew what and how to deliver instruction to students. The process allowed me to do it at my leisure, which I appreciated. As a teacher, you know we enjoy when we have autonomy over our own professional learning experiences. If you check out the National Board process, you will discover that it focuses on what students should know and do. The National Board candidates get an opportunity to demonstrate how they collaborate with students. You have autonomy over classroom implementations. Some states pay a small stipend for completing and accomplishing National Board.

When I went through the process, my district, state, union, and mentor supported me. I did not accomplish the National Board the first time, and I didn't question the process because I knew that I had some things to improve on. Like the other best professional development process, the National Board helped me focus on my instruction, students, community, and leadership. Claudine grew from the National Board process as well, and this is what she had to say about it:

> Completing and achieving National Board certification strengthened my practice and helped me achieve my goal of becoming an even more effective and impactful educator. As I speak with fellow educators, I regularly share

how becoming an National Board Certified Teacher (NBCT) helped me and my students. As an English teacher, I use rubrics to grade all of my students' written assessments. I'm not unique in this regard—having the rubric is a professional best-practice—serving as a guide for me and my students. Becoming an NBCT gave me a personal "rubric" to be able to evaluate my effectiveness as an educator, strengthening my daily work and making me more accountable.

I am now an ambassador for the National Board Professional Teaching Standards, and National Board continues to support me as a teacher leader. One example of their support was when I was a National Board fellow, and I received a chance to collaborate with National Board leaders and a cohort of other fellows. We met several times in Washington, DC to converse and work on projects. Each of us fellows had a great mentor to assist us with developing as future leaders with the National Board.

I am also a founding board member with some vibrant minority women in the NBCT Network of Accomplished Minoritized Educators, and I am a proud board member of the National Board for Professional Teaching Standards. I can't say enough how helpful these organizations have been in my life. I encourage you to check out the National Board Professional Teaching Standards website to learn more about pursuing the National Board process. It is indeed a life-changing experience that you can take part in at your own leisure.

Engaging in STEM

The Presidential Awards for Excellence in Mathematics and Science Teaching (PAEMST) are the highest US national honors for K-12 science, technology, engineering, mathematics, and computer science teaching. The Presidential awards can recognize up to 108 STEM teachers each year. The application serves as a reflection tool on how the applicants provide STEM knowledge to their students and motivate them to learn STEM.

When you apply, you can focus on just one STEM teaching area. Winning teachers receive an all-expense-paid trip to

Washington, DC, $10,000, and a signed certificate from the current president. Martha is proud to be a Presidential Award recipient not just because of the honor it bestowed but also because it opened networking doors for her and her school. "PAEMST allowed me to network with the National Science Foundation (NSF)," she said, "and through them, I was able to get some grants and good resources for my school." PAEMST is an amazing, life changing opportunity for STEM teacher leaders.

Joining Fellowships

Policy Fellowships

During my mid-year of teaching, I joined my first fellowship with Teach Plus. They gave me the chance to learn about significant issues in education through research, learning sessions, and collaborative planning with colleagues. While in the fellowship, I learned how to address problems and develop solutions. I also learned the importance of tugging on the heart of others to address issues; storytelling was a strategy that I learned to use in advocating for the profession. Teach Plus also provided me many leadership opportunities.

Since joining Teach Plus, I have been in several advocacy fellowships based on issues from policy to global connections. Fellowships train teachers and extend learning experiences to help them continually grow. If you can join a fellowship, do so; it is an excellent opportunity to foster a relationship with other like-minded educators.

Michael Dunlea reminds me of the America Achieves fellowship and the impact the fellowship had on us. We were provided several opportunities to travel and network with various organizations and government officials to advocate for change. We also were featured on NBC News Education Nation National Summit, Teacher Townhall Meeting held in New York City. It was a momentous experience. "In 2012, I was selected as an America Achieves National Teacher Fellow. This fellowship experience lasted for three years. During those three years, I met the most amazing and successful teachers and principals from across this country. More than 100 of the most diverse and most talented people in the field. I was inspired to become a better educator and a better human being by this group. I was supported by this group as I became a better educator. They encouraged and supported me on that journey. On the first day of the fellowship, I very much felt out of place. By the end of the three years, I felt that I belonged right alongside the rest of them. Having grown up in a very segregated area, I was very far behind in my understanding of the plight and truths of people of color in this country. The relationships that came out of this fellowship have opened my eyes to the realities of this country and the struggles that lay in front of my students and all students." As Micheal, I have grown personally and professionally, which helps me to advocate and address pressing issues that matter to me.

Global Fellowships

My global learning fellowship with the NEA Foundation was absolutely the best experience ever. Can you imagine seeing one of the seven wonders of the world? I had the chance to see Christ Redeemer in Brazil. Of course, I did not want to go because I feared heights, but many educators persuaded me not to miss that experience for my students. I went, and it was an amazing sight.

Then I was able to travel to South Africa to see and hear from students and teachers so I could learn about their education systems and challenges. While in South Africa, I had the opportunity to visit schools, see some amazing tourist attractions, and eat fantastic food. I also learned about their culture and traditions.

Wendy Turner and Michael Pope were with me in this fellowship and on this trip, and they agree that our time in South Africa was a fantastic learning experience that we will absolutely never forget. Michael Pope says, "The NEA Foundation trip to South Africa was transformational because it opened my eyes to the beauty of my people and gave me a thirst to return to find out more about where I originated from." We had so many emotional sparks on that trip, and we instantly wanted to do more for the profession and students.

Michael Pope also discusses the Fulbright Teacher Fund: "The Fulbright Teacher Fund was also transformative because it brought me to Japan and in the process, it allowed me to change a Japanese law and eventual move to Japan to teach. The Grosvenor's

Teacher Fellowship was also another wow moment as I travelled to Svalbard to look at global warming and was able to bring that back to my classroom to teacher conservation stewardship."

When applying for a fellowship, you should think about what you want to learn from the experience. You should also think about how you can learn and grow from that organization and how you want to impact student achievement because of the experiences the fellowship will lead you to have. Every time I go to a country outside of the United States, I think about what I can bring back to my students; I love collecting instruments and artifacts to share with my students. Bringing something home enables me to share my personal experiences and about the various cultures and traditions. After one trip, I created a lesson called "Sound All Around" that is posted on BetterLesson in which students learn about sounds by creating instruments that replicate the instruments I located around the world.

Be a Reviewer

Teacher leaders can be a reviewer in several ways such as textbooks, curriculum, assessments, and portfolios to name a few. Some companies and organizations that hire reviewers include ACT Aspire, SAT, College Board, Pearson, and Teacher Performance Assessment-Education (EdTPA). National Board for Professional Teaching Standards needs assessors as well. I have reviewed textbooks at the district and national levels. In reviewing books, I had the opportunity to evaluate texts and see if the textbooks were the best option for kids and teachers. EdReports gives educators opportunities to review textbooks on the national level, and I reviewed with them. When I first started, I received training in Chicago, Illinois. The training was intense, but it was rewarding because I understood how to critique textbooks. My colleagues and I had an opportunity to produce consumer reports to get suitable textbooks in students' hands. The experience was fulfilling because it challenged textbook companies to do what was best for kids, and that is always my goal: to ensure all students have the best resources and materials in their hands. Even if you are just starting out in teacher leadership and you want to do something at a distinct level, you can serve on a textbook committee. It is great instructional advocacy work. You can also be a reviewer for testing companies such as ACT Aspire, SAT, College Board, Pearson, or for Teacher Performance Assessment-Education (EdTPA). National Board for Professional Teaching Standards needs reviewers as well.

While attending graduate school, in Hattisburg, MS, I would leave during the week to stay with a friend, Jackson, MS., to review National Board entries. Being a reviewer, helped me to grow as a learner, but most importantly, support teachers with National Board.

Writing Curriculum

Once you're comfortable in teaching the curriculum, try writing some. Teacher leaders can write curricula for their districts or organizations. As you become an expert in your field, you can share your craft with others through curriculum writing. Being a curriculum writer will help your peers develop daily comprehensive teaching plans for their students. When you write a curriculum, you can powerfully share resources and materials that support student learning.

Joining Associations (and Other Professional Organizations)

Through associations and other professional organizations, teachers can apply for awards or grants and present at conferences. As a National Science Teacher Association (NSTA) member, I have applied for and received a few awards. Their awards were beneficial because I received a monetary prize, and I used the funds to pay for travel to their conferences and to cover the registration fee.

I encourage you to find an educational organization that can enhance your practice. You can sign up to receive newsletters where opportunities are posted for teachers. A quick visit to the organization's website will help you identify a chance to lead or volunteer within the organization as well. For instance, NSTA selected me to serve on the Shell Urban Development Committee as the chair and later chair and co-chair of the NSTA/Shell award. I helped select teachers to receive $10,000. NSTA and Shell gave us total autonomy for choosing the recipients of that award. NSTA continues to allow me to lead on panels, cohorts, and webinars. I am grateful for their commitment to teacher leaders.

Student Achievement Partners (SAP) is another organization that supports teacher leaders. They believe in providing equitable opportunities for all students. I am a core advocate, and I have the opportunity to serve on boards, present, and serve on panels. My career continues to soar because of SAP. You can visit their website to sign up to be a core advocate.

There are many organizations that provide leadership opportunities to teacher leaders. It won't be hard for you to find one that fits your goals and needs.

Applying to Inducted

The National Teacher Hall of Fame (NTHF) highlights educators who have served for twenty or more years in the profession. The application process allows you the opportunity to reflect on your career. Educators who receive this recognition are surprised in front of their school community and then visit the NTHF museum in Emporia, Kansas. The educators have a display set up in the museum to showcase their careers. They are in Emporia, Kansas, for a week to be honored and inducted into the NTHF.

The inductees also receive an all-expense trip to Washington, DC to be recognized by the NEA Foundation and other policymakers. They are given a ring, business cards, and other beautiful memorabilia. According to the NTHF, the organization's mission is to "recognize and honor exceptional career teachers, encourage excellence in teaching, and preserve the rich heritage of the teaching profession in the United States."

Martha Mcleod says, "The NTHF was wonderful in allowing me to meet Arne Duncan and discuss with him current issues in education at that time. Plus, two of the other NTHF inductees were also science teachers. We collaborated for a while, discussing things we were doing at our campuses and how we could improve on them."

Being inducted into the National Teacher Hall of Fame is a life-changing experience for educators! I was grateful to be inducted into the class of 2020! It was a dream come true! I love when other teacher leaders are highlighted for their exceptional careers.

Becoming a State Teacher of the Year

Each year, the Council of Chief State School Officers (CCSSO) provides a new cohort of State Teachers of the Year with one-year learning experiences while they celebrate each teacher. From the cohort, they select a National Teacher of the Year. Each state has a process for selecting its State Teacher of the Year. First, you have to be selected at the school level. Then comes selection at the district, regional, and state levels.

Wendy Turner was recognized as Teacher of the Year. This is what she had to say: "I will say that being a teacher of the year was transformative; I'm fortunate to be able to travel to many places, meet many people, take part in space camp, go through all the professional development with CCSSO, get media training, and learn about myself as I went through this year. You become an ambassador for education and learn more about policy and different pieces of the system."

They are several steps in becoming a state teacher of the year. If you are interested in learning more about being selected as Teacher of the Year, you can visit CCSSO or your district/state department website. The National Network of State Teachers of the Year (NNSTOY) is an amazing organization that supports teachers. State finalists can join NNSTOY too.

These transformational experiences will support and change you on the road to teacher leadership. They will broaden your horizon and expose you and your students to new opportunities. As you are empowered as a teacher leader, take the time to share special moments with your students and community. When you win, your students and community win!

Tips for Applying for Grants, Awards, and Memberships

In talking to a few teacher leaders and reflecting on what has worked for me, I discovered some key denominators that will help you succeed in completing compelling nominations, doing interviews, or seeking leadership opportunities. There will be times in your career when you have to share your story, so think of the following as a "portfolio checklist."

Get to Know the Organization

It is a great idea to get to know the organizations before you apply; start by exploring their websites. I recommend checking out their board members and reading their bios to learn about their goals and passions. Look at the organization's mission and belief statements to learn what they believe in as an organization. When writing an application, it is good to have concrete examples of how your goals align with the organization's goals. Additionally, if their goals do not align with yours, you may not want to connect with them or apply in the first place. If they have standards, such as National Board and Professional Teaching Standards, I suggest reviewing those standards as well. If you take time to learn about the organization, you will be in a good position to stand out.

Review the Questions Carefully

Just like taking a test, understanding the question is half the battle. The questions tell you what they are evaluating you for before you start the application. You should make sure you read the question carefully to make sure you have the right idea of what is requested from you.

While reviewing the questions, you can reflect over your practice to see if you have experiences that highlight moments in your class that address each question. Answer the questions completely; if there are three parts, answer all three parts. You want to submit a complete packet or portfolio. If you can't, then you have an opportunity to work on what is needed to complete an exemplary portfolio or packet. You also can work with a previous recipient of the award to discuss their interpretation of the questions. If you are required to do a virtual or face-to-face interview, it never hurts to ask for the questions you'll be asked before the interview. Some organizations will provide them. However, if they do not, in the interview, think clearly before you respond. Be your authentic self.

Be Honest

Sergio and Wendy suggest that you should be honest with your application. I agree with them. It is essential to share accurate information about your work. You want reviewers to see that you have completed the work and do not mind sharing what you do successfully. You must show integrity when completing an application. When you are recognized for your work, organizations may reach out to others about you, and you want the comments to align with your portfolio or packet. If you do the work, it is easy to share what you do. Honesty is key!

Focus on the Students

It is vital to focus on your students in your applications. As teacher leaders, our main goal is to make sure that we increase student achievement and positively change our students' lives. In your application, you should highlight what you do for students. Some questions you can focus on include the following:

- ◆ What do I do for students?
- ◆ How does what I do impact their learning?
- ◆ How do I address all the learnings styles of my students?
- ◆ Why am I implementing the strategies or methodologies that I do?

Sergio De Alba says, "The focus of every great teacher is to make a positive difference in the students they serve. If your focus is making a difference and can consistently improve students' success and give students hope, you will be rewarded."

Note: If you must submit a video, it is important to focus more on the students and less on you. Show the students engaged in a high-level instruction while you play the role of the facilitator. Make sure that you demonstrate what the portfolio is asking you for and that the video reflects the goals of the lessons. Let the students enjoy learning and don't get frustrated if they do something that was not planned.

As an illustration, I was recording my classroom for the Presidential Award. My students were collaborated in groups to determine what effect the height of an inclined plane would have on the distance a toy car would travel. One of my students wanted to test her pencil. Early in my teaching career, I would have been frustrated. However, on the video, I asked the students to make a prediction/hypothesis about how the pencil would travel. One said, "If the incline plane is high, it will travel a far distance." I said, "Let's tested it out!" She was so happy, and I submitted that portion in my video. Then, I addressed what happened in my packet.

Provide Specific Examples

I suggest providing specific examples of your work. You can share anecdotes of what students or other stakeholders have said or done because of your efforts. This is a chance for you to tug on the evaluator's heart. If they ask for videos or photos, share them so they can see what you do inside or outside your classroom. You want every opportunity to shine and showcase your identity as a teacher. However, make sure the examples you provide address the questions on the application. When you provide examples, you are taking the time to support your claims with evidence.

Share Milestones

You will have many milestones in your career as you continue to evolve each year. Keep the milestones coming by continuing to work on yourself as a leader, learner, and collaborator. Share your milestones in your application and show your continuous growth and development over time. It is always great to reflect on how you have evolved in a particular way or around a particular topic. If you have an opportunity to share what you're passionate about, do it! Share when you were inspired by new ideas and what you did to improve in the relevant areas over time. You know what you do well and what you have to improve for the benefit of your students or the school community.

Be Clear and Concise

Don't be long winded. Instead, be concise and fill the extra space you have with valuable content that sets you apart. If you write about setting goals or objectives for students, for example, talk share the strategies or methods you employ to address those goals. I suggest avoiding writing fluff—stuff that does not address the questions. Do not discuss things that you want to share because you want to highlight a particular accomplishment even though it does not address the question. Most applications have a word count, so take the time to develop your answers by addressing the questions.

Note: Most portfolios or packets ask for your accomplishments on your curriculum vitae/resume. So, take the time to highlight your career there.

Find an Expert Reviewer

It is a great idea to rely on a second reader (preferable an expert) who can provide feedback and check for clarity. I find it useful to receive feedback from other educators. In looking for an expert to review your application, try to locate someone who knows you and your work. They can aid you in making sure you answer the questions effectively or make sure you add things that are significant to your work. A friend who knows your work and is familiar with the organization or award you are applying to can be critical. Finding someone to mentor you who has been through the process is not impossible. Sometimes all you have to do is just ask. If they are not available, they will let you know.

Note: Ask for help, but do not expect your reviewer to take ownership of your work. A great mentor will guide you in the right direction by asking questions and giving you constructive feedback, not by doing it for you.

Follow the Rubric

Rubrics serve as a guideline for you to follow. To create a model portfolio or packet, it is essential that you review the rubrics and guidelines. The rubric and guidelines inform you on how you are scored. They also guide you and help you to develop an admirable portfolio or packet, since they measure the most important things about an application. I suggest looking at the rubric before and after to ensure each point is covered effectively.

Submit a Curriculum Vitae or Resume

It is important to maintain a current and professional curriculum vitae (or resume). A curriculum vitae outlines your academic and professional impact. Always keep your vitae updated and current to ensure others can easily see your efforts as a teacher leader. Many organizations request a curriculum vitae with each application so they can learn more about the applicants. Use your curriculum vitae as a tool to show a snapshot of your wonderful work as a teacher leader and as a reflection of your commitment to education. Since your vitae can continuously change, I suggest reviewing it periodically, making any necessary improvements, and saving it as a Google Doc (or somewhere else in the cloud). You don't want to lose your vitae because it can be challenging to remember your accomplishments and reconstruct the whole thing.

Compile Letters of Recommendation

Often, you will have to turn in recommendation letters or names of references to inform who you are as a teacher leader. The prompt will specify who these letters or references need to come from. When they write the letters or respond on your behalf, you can share some of the following information with one that is filling out your recommendation.

- ◆ Make sure the letter is current with the accurate date.
- ◆ Make sure that the letter is signed.
- ◆ Make sure that they address the letter to the appropriate organization.
- ◆ Make sure that they answer the questions provided.
- ◆ Make sure that they discuss your accomplishments (e.g., if you are applying for a science award, the reference letter should highlight your science work).

During an Interview

If you have an interview, you want to be prepared to make an impression on the interviewing team. Here are a few suggestions.

- ◆ Ask for the questions you'll be asked ahead of time because they may provide them to you.
- ◆ Develop your own practice questions.
- ◆ Create a mock interview team, so you can practice.
- ◆ If possible, leave a portfolio, pictures, or a brochure of your work with a focus on the students.

Finding New Opportunities

There are many wonderful opportunities available to teacher leaders—probably more than you know. Many of these opportunities present life-changing experiences for you to grow personally and professionally. Taking advantage of them will open doors for you, but sometimes the hardest part is finding the right opportunities to say yes to. Here are a few suggestions on how to discover and recognize the opportunities available to you.

Ask Your Peers

You can find many opportunities by conversing with other effective teacher leaders. Successful teacher leaders will naturally share various programs and organizations with you that have helped them. Your peers will likely inspire you by sharing their journey, and they can also connect and recommend you to organizations personally.

Research on Social Media

Many teacher leaders find opportunities through various social media outlets. Organizations commonly advertise teacher leadership programs on Twitter, Facebook, and Instagram. One of my favorite Facebook groups is *Scholarships, Grants and Summer Institutes for Teachers*. It is a private group, and they ask you a few questions before joining. The connections there are worth it. I suggest finding organizations online that support teacher leadership and following them so you can be among the first to know when they announce new opportunities. District and state department websites are great ways to discover grants and opportunities too.

Build Your Network with Intention

Joining the right networks can make all the difference. Many organizations disseminate newsletters or send them via email. In these newsletters, they share various leadership opportunities that they or other organizations offer. I have found several career opportunities by signing up for newsletters or joining the right organizations. For example, I learned about the Voya/NNSTOY fellowship on the NNSTOY website. I applied, and I was accepted into that fellowship. We focus on STEM education while new teachers collaborate with veteran STEM teachers. It is the perfect combination. Suppose you are not sure which organizations to join. I suggest talking to some successful teacher leaders. It is important to locate the organizations that meet your instructional goals.

Summary

Many organizations exist to support teacher leaders in their educational quest to impact student learning. These organizations provide training, networking, grants, and awards. Which opportunities you take advantage of is up to you. To find the right opportunities for you and to submit winning applications, reach out to successful teacher leaders for help and follow the suggestions in this chapter.

Stop and Reflect

- ◆ What organizations align with your personal mission and vision and could help (or have helped) you achieve them?
- ◆ Why is it essential to focus on students in any endeavor that you pursue?

11

Creating Your Own Opportunities

You can't become an effective leader overnight; it takes a lifelong commitment.

You might get lucky in your teaching life, but at the end of the day, some of the best opportunities of your career will be ones that you create for yourself. Creating opportunities for yourself is an attribute of the best teacher leaders, and like any worthwhile endeavor, it takes time and a lifelong commitment to learning. If you are committed to developing opportunities for yourself, you will see that it is worth the wait. Teacher leaders set goals for themselves, and they step out on faith to create new experiences.

Have you ever been on a roller coaster? Can you remember your first time? At first, you were probably unaware of all the twists and turns ahead; even if you had studied the track, you surely didn't understand what the experience of riding the rollercoaster would be like until you got off. Entering the world of teacher leadership can be like riding a rollercoaster for the first time. It can be scary and jaw-dropping because of the serious inclines or speed. Once you have been on the ride a few times, you are less fearful, and you enjoy it. You learn to anticipate what is going to happen next because you have become familiar with that ride.

As a teacher leader, I have served in many capacities (as a panelist, moderator, task force member, presenter, curriculum writer, etc.). Each experience felt like a roller coaster the first time but taught me something about myself or how to lead and prepared me for the next opportunity. Each experience empowered me to do more

DOI: 10.4324/9781003229537-14

for myself and my students. Once teacher leaders have learned from the various transformational experiences available, they are empowered to create their own "rides." They do not depend on others to develop or share their narratives. They become aware of their abilities to make a change inside and outside their classroom walls and are equipped with the knowledge and tools to do so.

Don't let promotional setbacks or a lack of a title convince you that you don't have opportunities to be a leader. During my teaching career, I wanted to be a mentor coordinator. I worked hard for the position and thought that I would receive it. However, it was given to someone else. At first, I was a little disappointed because I knew that I had worked hard for the position. Then I realized that I did not have to be given that position because I had other special moments to lead, and I could still mentor teachers informally. Also, it is important for other teachers to build their leadership capacity. As a teacher leader, it is important to share the wealth with other aspiring teacher leaders.

Teacher leaders grow through leadership experiences, and some of those come from opportunities they have created for themselves. They learn skills, knowledge, and dispositions while they are on such projects. Being on those projects helps to build their confidence and empowers them to be self-starters. They use the skills they learn to step off the ride safely to face their fears and create opportunities for others.

For instance, writing a book was a leadership opportunity that forced me to face some of my fears and share my leadership journey with you. There were times when I was nervous about writing this book; however, I know that I am capable of completing this and other challenging goals—and surviving the roller coaster ride, it has been—because of an experience that I had years ago.

While on one project, I and other committee members had to create a document for potential educators. The organization took the committee through a rigorous process to create a framework. We brainstorm possible standards to define what high school students exploring teaching need to know and be able to do to take their first steps on the path to becoming effective teachers. I am writing this book because of that process. While on my educational journey, I learned the importance of teachers' voices.

Ways to Create Opportunities

Throughout the remainder of this chapter, you will discover some common traits that I discovered regarding how teacher leaders create opportunities for the students and communities that they serve. Next are a few suggestions on how to start.

Embrace New Ideas and Innovation

Teacher leaders enjoy creating innovative projects for their classrooms or school communities. Through research, they keep abreast of all new strategies or methods. They also collaborate with stakeholders within and without their communities to support the needs of their areas. They develop ideas to implement the latest teaching techniques.

Martha Mcleod provides some insight on how teacher leaders embrace new ideas:

> Teacher leaders jump into projects that are 'out of the box' thinking ideas. For instance, I created a youth birding program at my elementary school in Texas which was the first of its kind as far as I know. This program has opened many doors of opportunity for me.

Claudine James says, "Designing student-led exhibits provides me with a unique opportunity to incorporate history, objects, and artifacts within ELA lessons. But most importantly, the exhibits help students develop self-confidence through enhanced oral communication skills, plus it inspires them to be civically engaged." Claudine creates opportunities where students can lead. In doing this, she is encouraging students to be current leaders.

Ask Questions about Everything

Teacher leaders know the value of asking questions to advance in the profession. They know that asking questions permits them to discover and make use of opportunities. They are inquisitive, and being inquisitive helps them to insert themselves in many groups. Don't give up if someone does not answer your questions because, eventually, someone will point you in the right direction or assist you as prompted.

When you ask questions, you will receive answers that are beneficial to you. Asking a lot of open-ended questions helps you learn from the experiences of others and makes clear how to implement others' good ideas. When you ask questions, you also feel more fulfilled and happy since you seek solutions to problems that you want to solve or gain a clear understanding of. Soon you will discover that it is not about the answers but the questions that make all the difference.

Michael Pope says it best: "Teacher leaders can ask questions in their networks about worthwhile, career-enhancing opportunities that may not be advertised in their local union or by their districts." When you ask questions in your network, you will receive the support that you are looking for. Don't shy away from asking questions on behalf of your students and school community.

When you ask questions, remarkable things come your way. I was once eating at a restaurant, and I spotted a local singer who was on American Idol. My students loved her, so I went over to her table and asked her to come to my school. To my amazement, she said yes. I took her to every classroom and the students were so excited. Throughout my teaching career, I learned that asking questions can be a rewarding way to impact students' lives.

Don't Be Afraid to Grow

If you want to create growth opportunities, be willing to get out of your comfort zone. Teachers tend only to do what is comfortable in their careers to avoid failure. I have been guilty of this myself. I have learned that when I open myself to trying new systems and opportunities, my approach changes for the better, and I am more successful.

"Participating in committees, attending conferences, fellowships, and working with others to make a difference provides personal growth and opportunities to improve your approach as an educator," says Sergio, and I agree. Pursuing growth experiences aids you in implementing successful projects more effectively. If you want your project to be a success, learn from the best how to do it right. Learning and growing is often uncomfortable, but working on yourself is always a great investment.

Pursue Advanced Degrees

When I completed my undergrad program, I was finished with school—or so I thought until I had my son. I had to find a way to support him. I looked at the district pay scale, and I found some promise in the salary I could receive even though it was not much. Then I saw how my father was moving up the educational ladder due to his advanced degree, and I remembered all the nights in my childhood when he would stay up late studying. I wanted to be just like him, so I said I could do it. I set my sights on becoming a principal.

I attended the University of Southern Mississippi, which was five hours away from my house. I had to make that drive multiple times during the summer to get back to my son. I was also going to Hattiesburg, Mississippi in the fall and spring. When I arrived for the first class, I stayed in my car talking to my mentor. I informed her that I was worried about being the only minority student in this program. Then I saw Kim. Yes! I was happy to see Kim because I did not want to be the only minority student in the program. In the beginning of the program, we would not sit in class together, since interracial connections were important to both of us.

It was tough going to school while teaching and taking care of my son, but the professional result was worth the sacrifice. When I completed the master's program, Kim and I discussed how glad we were to finally be finished with school. Then a college professor asked us to meet her for lunch. She asked us to return to get our doctorate degrees. I thought, "You want me to write a dissertation and take stats? Of course not!"

I went back first to get my Specialist in District-level Administration degree. Then, with much convincing, a close friend and my first principal convinced me to get my doctorate. Receiving my doctorate was an incredible experience, and it was doable because I was able to be flexible with the process as I was with the National Board Certification process. Even though I was already teaching in the classroom, I pursued these degrees because I wanted more leadership opportunities and because I wanted to learn how to effectively lead at the school, district, and state levels.

My degrees did prepare me for what I thought was the only way to lead: to be a principal or serve at the district level. I used to think that those were the only ways to be valued, have a title, and receive a higher income. I was wrong! Being a true teacher leader opens those same doors. Pursuing advanced degrees helped me become a teacher leader, and while I haven't been a principal or worked on the district level, I have had titles, advocated for policy and practice, and advanced in the field.

Obtaining an advanced degree may be a valuable part of your path to teacher leadership and can open many doors for you. If you are open to pursuing one, the most important thing you can do is consider why you want the degree, how it can assist you in your career, and how you will use it to help you grow professionally.

Connect with Other Teacher Leaders

Michael Dunlea points out the impact that connecting with others can have on your career: "The greatest way teacher leaders can create opportunities for themselves is by becoming connected to other teacher leaders around." Successful teacher leaders will likely be a key factor in helping you self-start a project. If you are looking for an opportunity, reach out to your colleagues!

Connecting with other teacher leaders is fun too. Personally, I enjoy conversing with teacher leaders who have created opportunities for themselves and others. In talking to them, I hear their challenges and successes along the way. It gives me hope that I can reach my own goals.

As Michael also suggests, "The best way that you can create opportunities for yourself is by creating opportunities for others. Over the years, I have been able to develop and nurture a network of like-minded teacher leaders that has led me to countless opportunities both paid and unpaid, but all have improved my skills as a classroom teacher." Creating experiences and opportunities for yourself is fun, but it is far more fulfilling (and rewarding in your career) when you share and give to others. I believe that doors continue to open for those who support others. Therefore, I always encourage teacher leaders to reach back and pull someone else up.

Be Reflective and Think Big

Teacher leaders know the importance of thinking big. When you dream, it allows you to envision and plan the world that you would like to live in. To create your own "why," you must develop a vision. You will then have to lay it all out to see in what direction you need to go in order to make your vision come to fruition. Most teacher leaders who innovate and start-up life-changing initiatives start by reflecting on what they are trying to change so they can center their innovative ideas around their vision. It is vital to visualize the path ahead so you can stay on course. Remember, it is sufficient to take small steps to make your project or goals come to life.

Opportunities You Can Create Today

I've seen many teacher leaders do remarkable things over the years to create opportunities and do good in the world. These teachers created their own "ride" by sharing their ideas and completing projects that benefited students—regardless of their current position. Here are a few examples to get you thinking.

- ◆ **Write books for children or adults:** teacher leaders publish books to teach students or share their practice and inspire other educators. Writing children's books can be a powerful way to support students' academic success.
- ◆ **Start an organization:** some teacher leaders have started their own 501c3 non-profits to extend their reach in education. They typically share their methodologies and curriculum with educators and support students' learning indirectly. Stephen Ritz started Green Bronx, which is changing the lives of kids and communities. Stephen says, "Currently, believe it or not, Green Bronx Machine

now touches 500 schools across the country. Additionally, we touch schools all around the world and will probably scale that up to 20,000 schools within the next five years."

◆ **Launch an educational website:** informational websites are a great way for educators to share their classroom practice with the larger world. Some teachers post videos of their classes, blogs, or share instructional strategies for stakeholders to view. Websites are an easy way to integrate technology as well.

◆ **Expand your social media reach:** Carlanda (The Magical Teacher) showed her Disney room theme on social media, and her video went viral. Stakeholders praised her for the time, effort, and money that went into creating an effective learning environment for students. The Magical Teacher was invited on the Kelly Clarkson Show to be recognized for her classroom climate and culture. Throughout my teaching career, I have seen several teachers doing amazing things with their students. I learned some strategies and techniques that I could implement due to their innovative idea. It is amazing how using social media can inspire others.

◆ **Organize a global project:** teachers collaborate with other teachers to bring teachers and students together around the globe. I once collaborated with an educator to create the Peace Sign Project. Students created kindness signs that represented want they wanted to see in the world after being engaged in a unit about well-known people who created peace in the world.

◆ **Keep a blog:** Michael Dunlea and I are bloggers for Edutopia. We use the platform to share our classrooms' best practices with others. Blogging not only allow for sharing but serve as a personal reflection space. Teachers love to learn what other teachers are doing.

◆ **Create a learning club or school-wide activities:** you can create a club for students in your school. The club can focus on the need of students and the school community.

◆ **Be a presenter or serve on a panel:** teacher leaders present at different conferences to share their practices.

Summary

Teacher leaders create experiences for themselves to benefit their students, school, and community. They think big and reach out for support as they open doors for themselves and others, creating positive change no matter their current title or position.

Stop and Reflect

- ♦ What is the next opportunity you will create for yourself or your students?
- ♦ What are you doing to continue to evolve in your career?

PART 4

Thriving as a Teacher Leader

12

Thriving Throughout the Journey

Don't just make it through your career; ignite your passion and enjoy it!

Let me tell you, being a teacher leader is not an easy feat. When you lead, you are in the driver's seat of your career. Like all car rides, there are times when the road is smooth and clear; you listen to your favorite music and enjoy the scenery. The ride is a pleasure. Other times, the road is bumpy and rough, traffic is thick, and you don't enjoy it as much. But even when the road isn't ideal, as you drive down it many times, you begin to learn the pattern. You learn to avoid the potholes and travel when traffic is light, and the grueling part of the ride goes away.

Being a teacher is challenging because you are constantly taking on multiple roles during and long after the school days. You frequently have to work with several people to get things done on top of your classroom work. No matter the roads they come across, learn to enjoy the ride. Their mission "is not merely to survive, but to thrive …"

In my career, I have hit some rough patches on the road to teacher leadership. There were times when projects fell apart, parents and students were upset, the administration challenged my thinking, my team members were not as committed as me, and so on. Sometimes these rough spots were of my own doing: maybe I did not communicate my expectations effectively, or I did not understand the other's expectations; maybe I didn't

DOI: 10.4324/9781003229537-16

communicate my vision. And some rough spots just came out of nowhere. I know combating rough spots can be overwhelming and stressful; opposition is difficult as a teacher, so this chapter is full of practices that have helped me and other teacher leaders love our jobs and keep from our lights shining bright.

Teacher leaders choose to lead the tasks, projects, and activities they do (often simultaneously) because they are fulfilled by leading inside and outside the classroom. They are committed to their students, their school, and their community. They are passionate about their innovative ideas, and they are committed to the work. They want to take additional leadership opportunities to assist for the greater good. Stephen Ritz believes "that you got to fall in love with doing something so hard that it stands a chance to kill you because therein lies the opportunity to change the world." Teacher leaders are passionate about their work and work diligently to create change in the world. Whatever you commit to in your career, make sure it is something you are passionate about and don't mind putting your whole self into the work.

Often, teachers wonder what they need to do to survive. I know that feeling, and I have been asked that question several times in my career. I love Stephen Ritz's response to that question: "I'm not surviving. I love life. Listen, if I'm in survivor mode, then I'm in the wrong profession, and I'm not saying the job is easy. I'm not saying that at all. I'm not saying this is a cakewalk, but I thrive. I thrive because I put myself in situations where I want to succeed, where I'm asking and making my expectations clear, and where people want me to succeed."

Stephen Ritz is correct. Teacher leadership is no easy walk, but you can thrive as a teacher leader by putting a few things in perspective. As teacher leaders, it is our goal to thrive—not just survive—in the profession.

Next, I'll share a few ways that teacher leaders thrive. There is no one perfect solution to the problem of trying to thrive in teacher leadership, so it is up to you to decide which suggestions resonate with you.

Build a Support System

All teacher leaders need a solid support system to make things happen for their students. This support system can be called on at different times of the teacher leader's career. It is the glue that holds everything together. Teacher leaders depend on the people in their support system, and those people are invested in the teacher leaders they support. When a crisis arrives, or when the teacher leader takes on an ambitious project, they know who to call on.

Claudine James says, "Teaching can be stressful, especially to novice teachers … When teachers feel supported, they can extend that same support to their students and relieve the stress that could cause them to quit the teaching profession."

My support system has been vital to me. One example is when school ended abruptly during the 2020 COVID-19 pandemic and classes were put on hold. Children didn't have devices to learn from home, the educational system was still trying to figure out how to continue online, and everyone was going into lockdown. While everyone was struggling to adapt, I reached out to my parents and my students to continue to engage them in virtual learning.

To motivate and encourage my students, I told them I would host an end-of-the-year celebration. I invited them to write their future plans for their school year and beyond. Students frame their plans to keep as a keepsake. Parents and students signed them. When the time came, we had our celebration. I decided that a virtual celebration wouldn't cut it, so we had a physically distanced ceremony on my front lawn. The students and their parents arrived dressed in their best attire, and I wore my cap, gown, and doctoral hood. A pediatrician (Dr. West) was on hand to ensure safety, everyone wore masks, and hand sanitizer was readily available.

I used the funds I received from the Harriet Sanford award, and some donations from my colleague/friend Adriane, to purchase mortarboards for each student and decorated them with the message, "Oh! The places you'll go!" A photographer friend of mine, Carlos, took photos to provide each child with a keepsake picture. My sister (Pam), who is a business owner, donated candy apples, and cookies. Also, I had a parent (Porchea), a school colleague/friend (Ariel), and some of my family members (mom, dad, and son) help decorate and pass out treats and food. I had two videographers (Trevor and Maigan) recording the event. As you can see, it took many family members and friends to make this event successful. I needed my support system because I could not have given my students this experience in the middle of the pandemic myself.

How to Build Your Support System

Rely on Family and Friends

Many teacher leaders are successful because of their family and friends. The people closest to you are lifelines for keeping teacher leaders going. Many families of teacher leaders take on the same commitment as the teacher leaders. They join in on projects to ensure that their family member (and his or her students) are successful. Teacher leaders share their successes and challenges with their families and friends. Family and friends provide advice on projects, and they celebrate teacher leaders' accomplishments. Teacher leaders need and appreciate their support.

I asked Stephen about his support system, and he shared this: "Number one, I'm blessed that my family has chosen to join me in this mission, and my wife left corporate America to do this. She left a tremendous job and an excellent salary to come and do this. So I'm forever grateful for her."

For teacher leaders who have kids, turning to family and friends is even more important. I was able to obtain my advanced degrees out of town because of my family and friends. They would watch and keep my son for me. I had one close colleague/friend, Erica, who would drive me to my son's Amateur Athletic Union (AAU) events so that I could rest. My son is important to me, and I must be there for him. Sometimes, I could call on my sorority sister, Jasmine to pick him up from practice. This goes both ways, of course. As a teacher leader, you must make time for your family and friends and support them when they need it.

Sergio says, "I ensure that credit is given to all involved for the success we achieve. Leaders cannot have success without the help of those around them; making sure that they are appreciated for what they do minimizes the challenges of leadership." Family and friends provide the love, support, and advice to keep teacher leaders going strong.

Who are the family members or friends you can depend on? Who do you need to thank for their support so far, and who do you need to strengthen your relationship with?

Develop a Small and Mighty Team

Teacher leaders develop teams to support their vision and mission. They understand the importance of creating groups to accomplish projects or activities, and that these groups don't need to be big. Stephen says, "You know how big my team is? My team consists of my wife, two consultants, and me. You don't need more. You do it with less." Stephens makes a valid point. A small team can be a mighty team and easy to manage. When you have a large group, it can be challenging to ensure everyone has a voice. You may lose some vital agents in the conversation, and some members may not be assigned critical roles if the team is too big. Building the right team will set you up for success, whatever the goal.

Your team should collaborate in small groups to discuss timelines and expectations and assign roles/responsibilities. As Martha suggests, "Delegate roles to members of a content team, and try not to do everything for everybody, or you will wear yourself out." Teacher leaders are often the lead contact or responsible party on the team, so they must be reliable and meet regularly with the team to keep them updated. Every team needs a coach to guide the team.

Note: The teacher leader may be the lead sponsor or chair of the group, but great teacher leaders make sure everyone is listened to and respected on their team, regardless of title. There is no "I" or "me" but "we" on the team. When the teacher leaders engage in professional development opportunities, they share what they learned with their group members so that everyone is on the same page.

Sergio says, "Everything I have ever proposed is based on what is best for students. Having this focus at the center of every decision makes it easier to gain the support of stakeholders. Additionally, I ensure that credit is given to all involved for the success we achieve. Leaders cannot have success without the help of those around them; making sure that they are appreciated for what they do minimizes the challenges of leadership."

Michael Pope makes a valid point: "You must build a strong teacher network of like-minded individuals who can build you up and inspire you, and you can do the same for them."

Leadership is a difficult job, and you cannot thrive without a good team. As a consequence, you need to pick colleagues who will complete the work in a timely manner to ensure the team runs smoothly.

Love Your Students and Show Your Passion

Teacher leaders love their students, and they lead with their students in mind. Teacher leaders keep showing up every day for the love of their students. They keep in mind the potential students have if they get an excellent education, especially the marginalized students. The world is competitive, and if students don't get an education now, they will be lost in our ever-changing society. Teacher leaders are aware that social justice changes things, so they ensure students have access to the resources they need regardless of their background. They fight systems that oppress students. They value students' voices and choices. They are accepting of them and encourage them to speak out on issues and solve real-world problems. In short, teacher leaders are the teachers they wished they had as a child; it is their goal to pay it forward.

Innovative ideas inspire teacher leaders' work because they see the effect innovation will have on the students that they teach. Majorie Brown says, "I enjoy talking with the students in the class about history and its role in current issues as well, and how everyone has a choice to be a perpetrator, resistor, bystander, or collaborator, in matters of social justice. I thrive on tackling social injustice and assisting pupils in analyzing power relations issues, seeing what changemakers can do, and how power corrupts. I think the humanities are essential in STEM to build thinking citizens who hold governments accountable." Margie is correct!

Remember to love your work. You may love some parts of it more than others, but whatever you love, focus on that. Love for your students and the lives they will lead should be at the forefront of your daily life. Beyond that, connect with issues and topics that you are passionate about and share them with your students.

Know Your Limits and Commit to What Matters

"Do you say yes over and over again, constantly spreading yourself too thin?" Knowing when to say no is an essential point that Michael Dunlea makes about knowing your limits. As a teacher leader, you must learn how to say no. Often, teacher leaders get overwhelmed because they take on too many tasks. Therefore, it is essential to prioritize your time and the things that you commit to. You can't do it all even though you may try. Before I commit to a project, I always ask myself a few questions:

- ◆ How much time will it take to complete this project?
- ◆ Will the students and teachers benefit from this project?
- ◆ Do I want to associate myself with this organization's beliefs and mission?
- ◆ What educational organizations or leaders are involved?
- ◆ Am I passionate about this project?

Those questions help me know what to say no to so that I can say yes to what matters most. It is critical that you associate with projects that matter to you and make the world a little better because you were at the table—you don't have time for anything else!

Seek Clarity

Have you ever been on a job where expectations were not clear? I have been there a time or two. I planned a project, and thought I understood what to do. Then after I've invested lots of time and energy into completing it, the person over the project informed me that it was not what they had in mind. My work was wasted.

Clarity is not always directly given, and it is something that you have to seek out. Before you begin any project or initiative, get to know exactly what is expected from the primary leader. If you are the one leading out, make sure you have a clear vision of your goal and communicate that vision to all others involved. Clarity helps eliminate distractions and saves time in the end. The effort it takes to get clarity is worth it.

Teacher leaders won't have to wonder what the person or organization wanted if all details are given upfront. You won't have to go back to the drawing board later because things were unclear. Related to clarity is transparency, which helps to reveal the unseen and establish relationships. Being a great communicator and listener is a great skill to possess when asking for or giving clarity. When you do a project at your school, it is a good idea to have checkpoints with the building-level leaders or organizations involved to make sure you're meeting their expectations. If they alter their vision halfway through the project, this is a time to channel your emotion positively. However, if you ask for expectations in the beginning, the rest of the project will run smoothly most of the time.

Here are a few questions to ask when you need clarity:

♦ What are your expectations?
♦ Do you have an exemplar model for me to view and follow?
♦ Can you provide a detailed outline?
♦ What are your goals?

Clarity helps to build transparency and helps nurture lasting relationships. It also helps to expedite projects and save you time. Seek clarity!

Take Care of Your Mental Health

Carlanda, The Magical Teacher, says, "I have to take care of myself. If I don't eat breakfast, then I'm not going to be magical because I'm going to be irritated. You have to know yourself, and I learned that during my first year of teaching. My kids started bringing me snacks, and it was so funny because I didn't eat breakfast. I started noticing every day that my kids were bringing me oranges and yogurts. I asked them, 'Why are you guys bringing me food?' 'We noticed if you don't eat, we don't have recess, or we don't know you,' they responded. That was when I noticed I had to sit back and reflect: how does my attitude affect the classroom? Teacher leaders have to make sure they eat. It always comes back to self-care. You must eat. You have to sleep."

Carlanda is right. Teacher leaders have to take care of themselves. If they are not good for themselves. They cannot be good for anyone else. Teacher leaders are often the last ones to be checked on because they seldomly complain—they are also frequently the ones checking on others. They are always multitasking and juggling responsibilities, and while they may seem invincible, they aren't. Remember to check in with the teacher leaders you work with. They may need you at certain times in their careers as you may need them.

Often, people ask me how I continue to burn the midnight oil. Well, I am always trying to find a work-life balance. I am not going to tell you that it is easy. But I can provide a few suggestions for you to consider as a teacher leader that will help you keep yourself healthy mentally and physically. Listen to your body; don't ignore it when it is sending you a message. Your physical health can impact your mental health.

- Make sure that you sleep enough. "Enough" is determined by you, but you have to rest to be an effective leader.
- Leave work at a decent hour. Your never-ending to-do list will still be never-ending tomorrow.

- ◆ Set boundaries and say no. It is okay to inform someone that you are not available.
- ◆ Do things that you love—that are not be school-related. Making time for a hobby, family and friend time, etc., will keep you passionate about life.

Detach and Recommit

Have you ever been in a relationship that emotionally drained you? No matter how hard you tried to reconnect to that person, you could not move forward. You had to take a mental and emotional break. When you walked away, you could think more objectively about the past (what captured your attention in the first place) and the present. Sometimes, these breaks make you miss those special moments, and you return to the relationship. Other times, you don't go back to that person because you no longer feel the same way.

There are times in a teacher leader's career when they need to detach from certain projects, people, leaders, and schools. They separate themselves because of issues at their job, loss of their passion or purpose, trying to lobby for a shift in policies and practices, or just because they need a break. It is essential to understand that just because you're a teacher leader does not mean you are married to a project, school, or administrator. If you do not see your situation as a good fit for you, it is fine to walk away to reflect. However, do not leave the profession because the students need you.

When you do take a step back, you should not do so without communicating effectively why you are leaving or need a break. It is a noble thing to tell someone why. When you tell your "why," you provide valuable feedback. Your comments can help someone else, so they don't get to where you are.

Within projects, plan breaks so you can take time to rest before committing to the following tasks. The educational world is constantly changing, and teacher leaders may shift their mindset depending on where they are and what comes their way. Sometimes, you tend to go where the opportunity leads you. When things just don't fit, and you feel that you made a mistake, be courageous and detach yourself. Acknowledge when something is not a good fit for you. When something doesn't fit you, it doesn't necessarily mean the project was wrong, just that it isn't right for you right now. When you walk away, you avoid permanent burnout. Your passion may return along with your energy and ability levels. If you recommit, your enthusiasm can come out in your teaching and leadership.

Overcoming Challenges

When the coronavirus pandemic first began, the school where I worked shut down abruptly. First, I worried this was a social justice issue that needed to be addressed—why were other schools operating online and ours wasn't? I had no contact with the parents of my students for about two weeks until one parent reached out to me, burned out and wanting to know what her child was supposed to do. I quickly contacted all the parents and asked them if they had devices that their child could use to connect to me online. If they did, I would meet with their child daily. We did the math, reading, STEM activities, Skype with Scientists, and had a virtual lunch with our New Jersey buddies led by a real-life chef. I would not let my students fail because of a pandemic, and I knew I needed to keep teaching and being innovative.

On the road to teacher leadership, there are many highs and lows. The art of being a teacher leader is all about how you deal with them. COVID-19 has caused many things to shift in the world and our classrooms. Teacher leaders learned how to maintain their classrooms while teaching remotely or in a hybrid format. They adapted and started teaching in a new way overnight.

We should not expect technology or the educational environment to stop changing. When faced with challenges, it is essential to stay calm and focus on what matters the most: the students. When you overcome challenges, you are motivated to do more—teacher leaders model pride for themselves and their students. Pride is a way to celebrate personal accomplishments. When overcoming a difficult situation, celebrating makes you feel like a winner while giving you the authenticity to model traits you hope your students will develop, such as perseverance, creativity, and problem-solving. Overcoming challenges is fulfilling and makes you want to do more, leading you to seek new opportunities to grow.

Summary

Being a teacher leader can be challenging and demanding because of the workload and many responsibilities teachers take on. Teacher leaders are committed to their students, schools, and communities. They want to create change in the world, but they cannot do that if every day is a struggle to survive. If teacher leaders are to continue their positive impact, they must discover ways to thrive. One of the key contributors to their success is support from family and friends. Ultimately, teacher leaders keep going for the love they have for their students.

Stop and Reflect

- ◆ What should you do to take better care of yourself?
- ◆ How do you overcome challenges?
- ◆ What makes you thrive as a teacher leader?

13

What We Need
Nine Things to Help Teacher Leaders Thrive

You have to be self-aware and observant in order to discover what needs to be changed.

In teacher leadership, you have to think about what you want to accomplish and what desires you have for teaching. Change cannot happen if you are unaware of the need for change. One reason teacher leaders thrive in the profession is that they are willing to advocate for what matters to them—they recognize needs and try to fill them. Teacher leaders dream big and share those dreams. They advocate for students and the profession. Sometimes, that requires advocating for themselves.

We all have the desire to share what we need more of or less of so we can feel fulfilled. Maybe you are looking for that perfect dress. Maybe you want a steak for dinner. Maybe you want a new companion. Maybe you want to eliminate some tasks from your plate so you can be stress free. Maybe you want social justice for all. In their jobs, teacher leaders also have needs that need to be met—things that keep them sane and loving their work. Whatever your needs and desires, voicing them is important. It's hard to *thrive* in the profession if your needs aren't being met.

DOI: 10.4324/9781003229537-17

At the school level, the administrator should find it more important than ever to listen to teachers. The recent pandemic has caused a shift in our educational ecosystem, and we need teachers more than ever to help students recover from the worldwide learning loss. As teacher leaders, we too often reminisce about the days when stakeholders ask what we need more of or less of so we can do our best work and thrive as teacher leaders.

What Teacher Leaders Need to Thrive

The only people who can tell you what teacher leaders need more or less of are those teacher leaders themselves. But speaking for the profession generally, my colleagues and I have developed a list of some hopes and dreams we hope will come true for teacher leaders everywhere.

More High-Quality Professional Development

Sergio Alba says, "The most significant factor for student success is a well-prepared teacher. My goal is to have students succeed; I believe more training is required to achieve this goal. Training should be engaging and developed by the teachers of the community being served. A practice designed without this focus creates sessions that do not support success or engagement from the teachers being trained."

Sergio is right. Teachers can sit in professional development sessions for hours and teach no better than they did before. A major focus in professional development is on the number of hours. It makes me think about my student teaching experience: I didn't see good quality teaching, but I got my hours in because that was the focus—quantity over quality.

Teacher leaders need schools, districts, and state departments to offer sessions that teachers need and that address specific issues instead of going with the one-size-fits-all approach. We push our students to be different by providing differentiated instructions and resources. Why can't we have the same philosophy for teachers?

There is no magic bullet to selecting the proper professional development material for all teachers. For instance, veteran teachers may not be as familiar with technology, so they may need more support in that area. New teachers might need help preparing engaging lessons or managing a classroom. The only way to know is to ask and then customize instruction. Teach to make up for individual weaknesses; don't assume everyone is in the same place. Teacher leaders need to have a voice in selecting their high-quality professional development, such as the National Board Certification process. Teacher leaders love to grow professionally, but they require high-quality, innovative instruction to continue to spark their creativity in their classrooms.

More Agency, More Autonomy

In the school setting, those closest to the students—teacher leaders—know the best way to support students. But they never really have the autonomy we need to support those students in all the ways they need. We are rarely asked what is best for us and our students. This is a mistake; teacher leaders' and students' voices are vital to successful education (and we should add family and community to that equation as well).

The teacher leaders are on the front line in that they are aware of students' and families' needs. We know first-hand when something is off because we have a daily personal connection to students and their families. Teacher voices are essential since they can help shape their work conditions and promote student achievement. As we reimagine education, it is vital for educational leaders to listen to their teacher leaders and use a bottom-up approach, not a top-down approach.

Too often, messages and plans from upper-level administration get lost and fall short when they get to the teachers, families, and students. The system needs the teachers, families, and students to lead out and do the work in order to improve education. Give us a voice and give us a choice. Trust teacher leaders to do what is best for students and they'll prevent wasted spending, time, and initiatives.

Teacher leaders are innovative and creative, and academic leaders can learn from them. Often, teacher leaders keep abreast with current issues better than those in higher positions. They keep current with leading ideas and collaborate with other organizations to impact change. Not only that, but teacher leaders are doing research on student success every day in their classrooms. Teacher leaders should be at the helm of the conversation about improving education.

More Resources

Teacher leaders need resources because it supports what we do. Often, teacher leaders spend their money out of pocket to provide for their students because what they are given is not enough. Innovative teaching provides students with an enriching experience, but it costs money to expose your students to high-quality resources. Some teachers have a rapport with families and organizations and can receive donations. In school districts facing poverty, parents don't have extra funds to send in supplies. There is a limit to how creative you can be without suitable materials. Historically, teachers have had to pay a lot to get the resources they need. Michael Pope says his school needs resources because teachers are usually required to provide their own. He is not alone. Teacher leaders need resources to help support their classrooms and schools' initiatives.

More Time

Teacher leaders yearn for more time to plan for the things that matter the most, but often teacher leaders must meet school and district mandates. Teacher leaders are engaged in excessive paperwork (i.e., typing minutes for grade-level meetings, grading papers, recording grades, completing data charts for students, posting data charts, writing short and long terms goals, recording interventions, filling out surveys, and so on). Also, there is a focus on the appearance of classrooms (i.e., anchor charts, accountable talk stems, posted objectives and standards, word walls with definitions, and classroom themes). While all of these aspects are effective measures for teachers, there is often not enough support provided for teacher leaders to accomplish these requirements as well as plan quality lessons within the confines of a work day.

Many teacher leaders feel guilty about taking time off since there are no subs due to the teacher shortage (especially during the pandemic), and they do not want to burden someone else. Teacher leaders rarely fully clock out because they are always thinking about their students and their goals to ensure that they learn every day. Teacher leaders often work outside their official schedule to implement programs and activities for their students. Martha Mcleod says, "I need more time to keep up with my programs and time to advance other meaningful programs with my students."

Though we cannot give teacher leaders more hours in the day, there are a few things administrators can do to support teacher leaders in safeguarding their time so they can focus on students and avoid burnout.

- Provide an uninterrupted hour in the day to focus on tutoring to reinforce skills or teach concepts.
- Protect planning time by establishing comp time or giving a half a day on a designated date for individual planning or team planning.
- Give teachers additional personal care days to support their mental health.
- Eliminate or reduce some of the duties of teachers.
- Offer teachers additional support in the form of co-teachers and educational teacher assistants for all grades.

Teachers need more time to build thriving classroom environments that meet the needs of all students. For teacher leaders, time is of the essence. In the next chapter, I will share how teacher leaders can better manage their time. Administrators can be strategic and intentional with schedules and assigning tasks outside of the classroom to help lighten the load teacher leaders carry.

More Support

Teacher leaders need more support from stakeholders. Time and resources are wonderful, but so is encouragement and willingness to contribute. With that kind of support, teacher leaders are empowered to complete tasks promptly and more easily overcome obstacles. Teacher leaders need their colleagues to support, and sometimes assistance, in planning and implementing projects. They also need managerial support to help deliver, and administrative support mitigates conflicts.

An important part of getting teacher leaders the support they need is acknowledging that they need support. It takes a team to make things run smoothly. Sometimes teacher leaders themselves need to be reminded of this.

Because teacher leaders need support from their district and community, it is important for both teacher leaders and administrators to build relationships with key players. The support of district departments can go a long way. For example, the Career and Technical Career (CTE) department helped me promote STEM education at my school. They provided resources and professional development training and continue to help me and my students thrive in STEM. I am so grateful for the relationship.

As Marjorie Brown stated, "Teacher leaders will have the space to try innovative plans in an environment of trust when support is provided. It gives teacher leaders a platform and opportunity to mentor other teachers." Great teacher leaders do not work in silos; they connect with a supportive team.

Less Redundancy

I was preparing to register for the summer semester of one year in graduate school. My advisor looked at my transcript and noticed that there was a course I had taken twice. I had no idea.

When I told my professor what happened, he asked me, "You didn't realize that you took the same class on two occasions?" I truthfully answered, "No," but I wanted to add, "I didn't notice because in every class I took from you, you wanted us to have the same book, and you told the same stories."

Along the lines of better professional development, teacher leaders need new and inspiring instruction. Sometimes, you have to sit and listen to the same stories or same protocols repeatedly. As Wendy Turner echoed, "Time is valuable." Teacher leaders should focus their time and energy on doing more for kids or themselves. If a piece of instruction is something teacher leaders have already heard a dozen times, it's best not to give it. We tell our students not to repeat themselves when writing or think about ways to present their ideas in a more simple or interesting way. We should surely do the same at the professional level, so we spend our time in more valuable ways.

Less Isolation

As the old saying goes, "It can be lonely at the top." Teacher leaders too often work in isolation to accomplish their goals. That can cause them to feel lonely and isolated. When the last student leaves the building, the teacher leader is still there. When the last team member leaves the meeting, the teacher leader is still there. Many people don't notice the sacrifice and focus instead on the title or position a teacher leader has. When peers or teacher leaders do this, the result can be professional jealousy. Instead of being viewed as an asset, teacher leaders can be viewed as a threat by those they work with. This only widens the gap between them and teacher leaders and increases the isolation those teachers feel.

Majorie Brown says, "[teachers] also need to have support structures beyond school, as many schools or colleagues could feel threatened by teachers who go the extra mile and who potentially show them up …. teachers need to persevere with colleagues and be inclusive in their activities. Also, be open to new teachers who may be keen to learn and be mentored—be open to engage with whoever expresses interest. Don't be dragged down to the average level acceptable to the many—be resilient and aim for what you believe in."

Wendy Turner says, "As I remain grounded in students and helping others, [being viewed as a threat] is disheartening. However, with empathy, I realize where this is coming from and, using my own SEL competence (self-awareness and self-management), it challenges me to figure out how to nurture and create positive relationships when this happens."

Ideally, the people who are doing the work should be supported and rewarded by their peers, not envied. If a person shines their light on the world by sacrificing their time and energy, everyone should appreciate them. That appreciation creates connection and helps lessen the fatigue of leadership.

Those who envy or criticize teacher leaders often don't understand the hard work that goes into the job. Only a few members of the audience know, if anyone, everything that goes on during a dramatic or musical production. Similarly, the teacher leaders are always backstage, making sure that everything is ready before they showcase their work or show up for students. The backstage part is the part others don't see.

Michael Dunlea suggests, "There needs to be more consensus throughout the profession that we're all working towards the same goal to promote less resistance among colleagues." Colleagues should support one another. We teachers need an environment of connection, not isolation. We should celebrate each other's successes and dreams, not each other's failures. Our students, prospective teachers, and the community at large need us to show them the way.

Less Micromanagement

Teacher leaders need to be trusted to do their job. There is no need for micromanagement or "power tripping." Teacher leaders are intrinsically motivated and pride themselves on completing their job successfully. It does not take people in authority to stand over teacher leaders and monitor their every move.

What teacher leaders do need from management is checkups where the administration offers support and asks what could be done to make the lives of their teachers easier (teacher leaders hardly ever complain, so it can be hard to tell when one needs support). Contrary to what seems to be popular belief, micromanaging does not make teacher leaders work better. Often, district leaders put pressure on the administrators. Then they put pressure on the teachers. Then the teachers put pressure on their peers and students. This becomes a trickle-down effect that causes burnout on all levels. When people burn out, they check out. No one is reaping the benefit of a successful school system. There is a high turnover rate among teachers and lower test scores among students. The goal of the system should be to retain teachers and create an environment that has less authoritative actions so teacher morale can increase and students can get back to learning.

Less Busy Work

Teacher leaders are industrious, and they want to do a great job! They voluntarily do additional work for the love of the profession and students. They volunteer their time to give to their students, families, colleagues, school, and community. However, the most valuable activities a teacher can do are frequently jeopardized by unimportant but urgent tasks. With less busywork, teacher leaders will naturally spend their time on more essential things.

Martha Mcleod makes a valid point when she says, "I need less time with busy work stuff that has no impact on a child's learning or education. Meetings and protocols are time zappers in a teacher's busy day and hinder the time I can spend on quality learning projects with the students. Teacher leaders would love to spend their time building better global citizens for tomorrow. Those learning experiences take time to plan and execute." As much as possible, teacher leaders need to be freed up to do what they do best: teach.

Summary

Most people sense problems within the educational system but are unaware of what those problems are. Listening to teacher leaders and promoting teacher agency is the first step. Teacher leaders love to do quality and impactful work, so supporting them is the key to improving education. If unhindered by unnecessary requirements, activities, and micromanagement, and if given the resources they need, teacher leaders will naturally work to create positive change in the lives of their students.

Stop and Reflect

- ◆ What do you need more of to thrive as a teacher leader?
- ◆ What do you need less of to thrive as a teacher leader?
- ◆ Why is it essential to promote teacher agency?

14

What to Do When You Don't Have Enough Time

Everyone wants more time but doesn't know how to use it wisely.

"I am swamped, but I love everything I do," Majorie Brown told me. Can you relate? There never seems to be enough time in the life of a teacher. Many teacher leaders devote their time and energy to their school and students, but we know that time is limited and that there is not enough time in the day to do everything that we have to or want to do.

Have you ever wondered how to accomplish certain goals with a limited amount of time? I have pondered over that question several times. When I was working on my doctorate, leading several projects at school, teaching, being a mom, and participating in several organizations, I wondered how I could possibly thrive as a teacher leader. One reason I was able to make it through that time in my life was that I had support. Another reason was that I learned to manage my time.

Stephen Ritz tells us that, "TIME stands for a Thing I Must Earn. Therefore, I'm very guarded with it in some ways, and very generous with it in other ways." Michael Dunlea says that "time management is a very tricky situation for teacher leadership." Time is indeed a tricky situation for teacher leaders because we don't have enough to do the things that we are passionate about.

DOI: 10.4324/9781003229537-18

Most of us are poor time managers, always wishing we had more time to make up for it.

Majorie Brown told me that one of her ways to get more out of her time is to focus on what she's passionate about: "I get energized by meaningful activities—they make me feel alive and relevant," she said. "I would encourage teachers to find their passions at school and get to know pupils beyond the classroom. You see them in a different light. I do extracurricular activities at schools, such as transformation and Model UN. I also am involved in National activities, such as a Women's History collective, the SA Society for History Teaching of which I am president, and international activities such as the Climate Action Project, Teach SDGs, etc. This makes me feel rooted in my school, country, and yet a global citizen."

Marjorie's passion drives her, and she is willing to give of her time to devote to her school and country, South Africa. Not only is she willing to do so, but by putting what she's passionate about first, she ensures that she has energy for the most important part of her job.

I have learned a few time management pointers of my own along the way that are backed up from the experiences of a few of my favorite teacher leaders. The rest of this chapter will give you teacher-to-teacher advice on how to better manage your time.

Prioritize: Now or Later

Something that helps me is dividing my tasks into two categories: now and later. This is a way of prioritizing your activities by their level of importance. The most important things should be done first—now. The less important things can be done later. One way to do this is to create a to-do list with "now" or "later" written by each task. Another way is to have two lists, one full of things you need to do right now and another full of things you don't have time to do now but that you don't want to forget about.

Martha says she manages her time in the following way: "I manage my time by taking care of my necessities first such as getting quality hands-on labs set up in my classroom. Non-essential stuff can wait until the next day. I try to have every little thing completed in a day."

It is okay if you don't get everything done in a day that you were hoping to accomplish as long as you spent your time on the most important items. You can always return back to your list the next day. Try to avoid multitasking, so you can give your full focus to what is important. By focusing and doing one thing at a time, you can work through your list efficiently and move on. It is vital not to let things pile up. Setting small deadlines for yourself can aid as well, but this suggestion may not work for everyone. You have to create a timeline that works for you.

Like Majorie Brown advised, an important part of time management is doing things you enjoy and that you feel are making an impact. It's hard to get through a list of boring things, no matter how well you plan your effort. Teacher leaders know that they thrive because they are involved in passion projects. They make time for those things outside their normal school days. And when things happen that you did not plan or have control of, remember to focus on your passion and avoid others' challenges.

Note: It is helpful to create a daily plan to eliminate or avoid stressful moments.

Clock Out

Teacher leaders often clock in, but they rarely clock out of their jobs. Be that as it may, it is important to "clock out" and find time for yourself. Teacher leaders need to turn it off in order to regenerate. They must take the time to shut down to have energy. Setting limits when working with others helps to safeguard time. It is helpful to tell others how much time you can spend or give them. Remember, teacher leaders have office hours, and you do not technically have to work outside them. Now, you may make expectations to this rule, as most teacher leaders do. But you can (and should) set a cut-off time. If you arrive at school an hour early, leave on time. If you arrive on time, stay an hour after school, but not more. Carlanda discusses how she arrives early to school to plan out her day. "I get to work every day at 6:30 am. School doesn't start till 8:00 am, but I get there at 6:30 am because I want to set up my room up and I walk through my lesson. I read the text that I am going to read for the day."

When you are off, you are off. There are times when teacher leaders have to leave work or projects unfinished. It is fine to ask for additional time if needed. If you do not get the sleep, family time, or creative rejuvenation you need, you will deprive your students and your projects of your best effort, and you will not be your best self.

Take Breaks from Social Media

"Teachers really want to have a big social media presence," says Stephen Ritz. "I don't know why, but I think it's important to put your feelings and facts out there for whatever reason. But less time on social media is probably the best thing you could do."

Social media has become a marketing tool for teachers and a place to showcase their accomplishments. They post about their practices, students, ideas, and views on social media. Many people are inspired by the work that they do. However, teacher leaders can easily spend too much time on social media. People who use social media can spend hours throughout the week strolling, posting messages, or posting pictures. Many people who log the time they spend on social media discover that they have a large portion of time they can devote to something else. Throughout my career, I have taken a break by deactivating my FaceTime, since I spend lots of my time there. I took a month off, and I realized that I had additional time for other projects and students. I maintained my Twitter account and Instagram, but I did not use those accounts. Another approach is to dedicate only a certain amount of time to your social media account each week.

Set Boundaries and Focus on You

Wendy is a great example of using her time proactively. "I know when I'm best," she says, "I have a much better flow in the morning. So I get up at five every day, and I prioritize exercise. If I don't do that, things aren't going to work for me. Then I work a lot. But I have certain boundaries for myself. So I come home after school, and I will always have a cup of coffee, watch TV shows, and sit and relax at home. I don't want to work right away, but I know I have some work to do, so as long as I can chill for like an hour or two, I'm okay to work a little bit later on. I try to make a rule to never work on Saturday because I am depleted on Friday. I go to bed early, though, so my flow in the morning is better. That's part of my feeling confident, so I'm going to get more done earlier in the day, and I'm going to pretty much shut it down and shut it off at ten. My home also deserves my time instead of being put on the back burner."

Wendy knows that it is important to focus on her and her family, so she can be an effective teacher leader. It is essential as a teacher leader to safeguard your time for yourself. *You are important*, and you need time to love and enjoy yourself. If you are not good, you can't be good for anyone else.

Stephen Ritz suggests that teachers focus on, in his words, "What squeeze gives you the most juice. And if not, how can you be most effective? You can't be all things to all people. So you've got to be best to yourself. And that's guarding your time." Stephen makes a great point! It is vital to consider how you want to spend your time, so it is good to set boundaries and focus on yourself.

Work Smarter, Not Harder

Here is Michael Dunlea's advice: "It is so critical that you do not overextend yourself. I always think of the phrase, 'Work smarter, not harder.' And never do something that doesn't bring you joy. The weight of a joyless task is ten times that of one that gets you joy."

My philosophy is to keep it simple. Sometimes, people feel that working hard or putting a lot of time in a task is the only way to get fulfillment from the work. But being simple can sometimes be just as good. Try not to overthink things because overthinking can make things more complicated and require more time. I suggest that you trust your gut instinct.

Developing a great team can also help you eliminate your workload. I enjoy working with others to get a project completed. If you lead the project, delegate assignments to help you spend less time. This isn't you freeloading on the effort of others, of course; it's about everyone pulling equally. It is vital to get people on your team who are willing to devote just as much time as you to the project. It is not fair to depend on someone doing 100% of the work, especially if all team members are receiving credit for the project. Micromanagers are also bad for the team. They will only make the tasks harder and strain the relationships. So, delegate to committed people and trust them to get the job done.

Organize Your Emails

Teacher leaders receive an enormous number of emails from stakeholders. It takes time to go through each email and to read and respond to each one. If you are trying to cut down the time you spend reading emails, consider creating folders with the words "now" and "later." If you can wait to respond to an email, do so. The ones that need your attention now can be answered at your earliest convenience.

Stephen Ritz says that he receives several emails a day and he only looks at the ones he needs to respond to. Additionally, give yourself permission to not check your emails after a certain time. That will give you some dead time. Gmail has several features to assist with organizing emails as other platforms. For instance, Goggle allows you to put stars by each account. You can place a star by the most important account. And don't feel the need to answer all your emails. Not all of them need your attention. Deleting and decluttering your email account can help you avoid getting lost in your inbox and losing track of time.

Keep Track of Events

Teacher leaders should keep track of their events effectively to ensure that they keep up with meetings and tasks. Another reason they should keep track of their events is to avoid overbooking their time. I like to use my cell phone to save events on my calendar. Google and Microsoft Teams are great for receiving alerts and reminders. You can also try posting multi-calendars at home or work to serve as physical reminders. Some teacher leaders like using a planner for writing dates and notes. There are also many mobile apps designed to help keep track of time. Find something that works for you! If your schedule is clear, organized, and manageable, you'll be able to meet each day with a level head.

Summary

Teacher leaders must treasure their time and use it wisely. They must consider ways to make time for things that matter. It is not an easy feat because there is never enough time in the day to do every good thing they want to do. Teacher leaders find ways to create balance in their schedule and on their to-do list so they can savor the special moments in life and do their best work.

Stop and Reflect

- ◆ In what ways do you manage your time well?
- ◆ In what ways do you manage it poorly?

PART 5
Developing Teacher Leaders

15

How to Champion Teacher Leaders

You have the patience and passion to make your dreams come true.

You have the power in you to change lives—and even the world—by becoming a teacher leader. Once you have done so, your next challenge is to identify and champion others on their path to teacher leadership.

Giving back by mentorship is an essential part of teacher leadership because no one can become a teacher leader in a silo. Just as others have helped you in your journey, you should help those who have not made it as far as you have. When you walk through a door in your career, hold it open for the next person. Opportunities beget opportunities in the profession, teacher leaders train developing teacher leaders, and the cycle continues. Continuous and intentional development is needed or the educational system risks running out (and falling apart) as future leaders—among teachers and students—disappear.

Giving is always worth it. Not only does giving bless your life, but you can unlock the greatness good in other people and in yourself by doing so. Leadership comes from the understanding of the importance of building other leaders—the more, the better!

Of course, leadership does not only happen with those who help train teachers in the schools to become leaders. Principals

DOI: 10.4324/9781003229537-20

and teacher leaders can collaborate alongside each other to gather to improve the educational landscape for all teachers. Everyone in the profession has a role to play in discovering teacher leaders. No matter what role you currently have, I encourage you to look for potential leaders whom you can encourage; encourage them to lead in their homes, schools, and communities. The generation of leaders are out there waiting to be discovered by you! Always remember that great teachers LEAD!

This chapter will teach you how to attract and support the teacher leaders who will join forces with you to transform your school and community. Now, let us take a close look at how to Locate, Educate, Acknowledge, and Demonstrate (LEAD).

Locate

How do you locate potential teacher leaders? I'm confident that there is a teacher leader who is waiting to be discovered by you. They are in your school building, your district, or your state. They may be following you on one of your social media accounts. They need your support and you need theirs! They need you to find them so they can advance in the profession. You need them to lead out in their school and community for the next generation of students. Their passion must be discovered, and the torch of opportunity must be lit.

Here are a few practical strategies to help you find the teacher leaders you are looking for.

Grow Your Teacher Leader Pipeline

There are schools with talented teachers in their buildings and in their communities. They are bright and ready to learn more about how to lead in their respective schools. Some of these teachers you will find already in their teaching career. Others you might find when they are still in school themselves. If you can discover them when they are in high school, college, or early in their careers, you can set them up for years of success as a teacher leader.

Developing a system for identifying potential teacher leaders before they establish themselves in the profession will give you a pipeline of leaders for your mentorship—and some of the best may even end up working at your school. You should not have to go far to discover these individuals because you can start with the students in your own school. By teaching your students to lead—no matter their age—you will inevitably inspire some who will be in the next generation of teacher leaders. You can be that potential teacher leader mentor and their lifeline on their teacher leader journey.

Stephen Ritz says, "If you are not growing and recruiting local talent, you are destined to die. You are destined to be on that hamster wheel of looking for people, chasing people, looking for people, chasing people … people should not have to leave their neighborhood to live, learn and earn in a better way. And if we look to ourselves for the best talent and we look to ourselves to nurture that talent, that talent will remain where it needs to be—with us."

Work with administrators and teachers in your school to design a long-term pipeline for inspiring and connecting with future teacher leaders.

Host Teacher Leadership Fairs

Most teachers sponsor Career Fairs at their schools, but seldom do they feature their own careers. To encourage and motivate the next set of teacher leaders, it is vital for you to showcase your life as a teacher leader. Teacher Leader Career Fairs are great places for teachers to share about their careers. They can show visuals or videos so potential teacher leaders can see their journey in action. They can also encourage questions from their students and potential teacher leaders about their job. These fairs can also be hosted at your schools or districts. During the fairs, you can invite prospective teacher leaders to fill out an interest form and reach out to them to meet one-on-one or in a group to learn more about the roles they want to play or learn about as a teacher leader.

Recruit through Social Media

There is power in social media to reach people. You can inspire the next group of teacher leaders by showcasing your work on social media channels. Also, you can post positive messages encouraging them to lead at different levels. You can start a campaign telling them that you see them as next teacher leader. If they hear it enough, someone will catch on.

McDonald's has this catchy phrase: "I'm Lovin' It." It is so catchy that after you watch the commercial, you find yourself repeating the phrase and wanting something from McDonald's. If you don't like McDonald's or never tried McDonald's, the phrase may, over time, convince you that maybe you want to try it. The same thing can happen with a teacher leadership campaign. Teacher leadership needs to be marketed too, and it can happen by you authentically sharing about your work. Don't stress about instant results; be consistent, and with time, you will reach the right people.

Leverage Referrals

Have you noticed a potential teacher leader in your building and spotted them doing something great, someone who seems like they might have a special interest and ability for leadership? They stood out, and you caught them doing great work. If you have, then your next step should be to refer them for leadership positions at their schools or districts.

There is a possibility that the potential teacher leader is looking for something more in their career. Can you imagine how they will feel receiving an email complimenting them on their work and informing them of an opportunity waiting for them? When I first started teaching, I remembered my first principal referring me for a role at the district level. It was the best feeling in the world to be recommended by her.

By referring potential teacher leaders for leadership positions, you can champion them by putting them in places where they can use their influence on a larger scale and grow in teacher leadership. On the other side of things, you can also ask for referrals from others in the profession, and when they spot potential teacher leaders, you'll be one of the first to hear about it.

Host a Potential Teacher Leader Meet-Up

Fellowshipping is a great way to discover and bond with potential teacher leaders. It is therefore essential to create opportunities for potential leaders to network and engage with teacher leaders. Creating a space for conversation promotes relationships and brings people closer together. You want potential teacher leaders to feel comfortable, so you should think about creative ways to talk to and learn from them.

You can provide a meet-up location that is inviting to the potential leader. Think about a catchy theme or name to capture their attention such as "Sip with a Teacher Leader," where they are invited to bring their favorite mugs with a quote on it that describes them, and you can create a conversation around that mug while learning about them. Then you can provide an opportunity for them to learn about you. Also, you can share beverage drinks or hot chocolate with them. You can also host a "Teacher Leader Lightning Round Session." You can invite other teacher leaders and have them sit at a table and allow potential teacher leaders to rotate table to table to network in a timed environment, much like speed dating.

Do whatever you can to attract that future teacher rock stars. These events don't have to be limited to teachers either; you can invite other leaders to the event such as building-level principals or district leaders. This will provide potential teacher leaders with even more exposure to the profession.

Ask Them Questions

In teaching, we tell the students to ask questions because we know that questions are powerful. Questions permit you to acquire knowledge and learn about an individual—what they are thinking, how they process things— and eliminate confusion. We should certainly ask questions from potential teacher leaders. But we should also ask questions to connect with them, just like we use them in teaching to connect with our students. I think that it is important to ask the teacher leaders questions to get them to consider leadership roles or discover if they are interested in teacher leadership.

When I was on an interview team once to hire a second-grade team member, I remember asking her questions to see if she had the desire to be a teacher leader and the potential to collaborate on projects together. One question that I asked was, "Are you willing to work outside the school day?" When I talk to her now, she reminds me of her answer to my question that day. She said she knew that she had to devote additional hours beyond the school day to do her job right. Now she is a co-chair with the STEM Club and she serves in other leadership capacities (reading laureate and on the instructional leadership team). Questions are powerful!

In working with Marjorie Brown, she and I developed a list of questions you may ask during one-on-one time with potential teacher leaders. Note: I would only select a few questions, since you do not want to overwhelm them and turn your conversation into a job interview.

◆ What do you think the role of a teacher leader is?
◆ What is the importance of thinking flexibly, finding humor in all things, and thinking interdependently, as attributes of educators?
◆ Can teachers be change-makers?
◆ Are you willing to spend additional time working outside the school day?
◆ What keeps you up at night?
◆ How does a teacher maintain one's personal life and help shape the lives of students?
◆ Can teachers transform communities? If so, how?
◆ What are your leadership qualities?
◆ Do you see yourself as a leader? Why or why not?
◆ How can I support you?

After the session, the developing teacher leaders will have an opportunity to reflect over their career. They will leave thinking about if they are ready to travel up the road to teacher leadership. Also, the leadership teams will have an opportunity to see those in their building or district desire to be teacher leaders.

Tap into Unrealized Potential

Some teachers are around you and have the potential to be teacher leaders but do not show up on your radar. Some of them think that they are not ready for teacher leadership; they have not developed that confidence. Sometimes, we see potential teacher leaders doing good things, but we do not know their full potential because they've never been given a chance to do great things. We tend to focus on the highflyers—the ones we see leading in their classrooms. However, we must provide opportunities for all teachers, just as we do for our students. We can't assume what someone is willing to do or capable of doing without asking them about it.

It is vital to tap into these overlooked teachers' potential for leadership. Teachers may leave if they don't see a way for them to grow or that anyone believes in what they are doing. Teachers are always trying to do what is best for kids.

Michael Dunlea gives the perfect example: "I had a teacher assistant who had a great connection with the students. She was exceptional talent with the kids. I was doing the planning, and I was not aware she was so creative in planning until she began to teach down the hall. We became friends, and she was sharing her plans with me, and I could see her creativity with designing lesson plans." It is important to give people opportunities, try to step out of their way, and let them lead. If we get out of the way, we can see how good potential teacher leaders are in action. You do not want to miss out on someone who has the potential to lead, so take a gamble on presently unrealized potential.

Recruit Minority Teacher Leaders

As a teacher leader of color, I had the opportunity to experience several amazing, life-changing moments. Those experiences made me a better teacher for my students of color. Seeing is believing and it is important that people see themselves within the people that are leading and being successful. However, in the beginning of my career, I did not see many teacher leaders of color in leadership roles. Often, I was the only one in those spaces. I wished there were more, so this became an area in which I advocated for more diversity in different opportunities.

According to the National Center for Education Statistics, "In 2017–2018, about 79 percent of public-school teachers were white, 9 percent were Hispanic, 7 percent were black, 2 percent were Asian, 2 percent were of two or more races, and

1 percent were American Indian/Alaska Native." There were
48.1 million students in American schools that school year;
22.0 million were white, and 26.1 million were minority students.
In looking at our racial dynamics, there was a disparity among
our teachers and students.

More minority teachers are needed to work with our minority
teachers. It is valuable for minority teachers to be recruited
as teacher leaders, especially with a high focus on Hispanic
and African-American teachers. Minority teacher leaders can
inspire their minority colleagues, students, and community to
pursue teaching careers. Teacher leaders can equip our minority
teacher leaders to lead in their school communities. Seeing more
minority teacher leaders will inspire more members of minorities to pursue a teaching career.

There is a great benefit to training minority teachers to be
teacher leaders. They can influence their community and the
students that they teach. When students of color see people who
look like them, they can more easily succeed in and out of school.
There needs to be an opportunity where students of color see
teachers who look like them leading. Teacher leaders of color
relate to students of color, and they help to uplift marginalized
students. Diversity can also help eliminate bias for minority
students and teachers. Let me share with you what a few of my
colleagues had to say about the importance of recruiting minority
teachers.

Stephen Ritz says, "Black lives matter. Let's put it out there,
and we need to say it, and we need to mean it. I'm a big believer
in inclusion and diversity, and I like the rainbow mosaic, so to
speak. More minority teacher leadership. Listen, you don't have
to be a weatherman to know which way the wind blows in communities of color and poverty. If there aren't opportunities for
leadership for people of color at the top, it's never going to attract
people of color to pursue teaching."

Sergio Alba says, "I am a Mexican American. My parents
were both farmworkers from the same region in which I teach.
The fact that I am their teacher is a daily reminder that, as my
mother always says, 'It doesn't matter where you come from,
what matters is where you want to go.' I am a daily example of

the possible and the message that I am sending cannot be made in words. The example of the possible can become the difference in how students see their own future."

Recruiting teacher leaders of color can influence our school communities. It is vital to recruit a diverse group of leaders to help create positive paradigm shifts. Claudine James says, "This definitely is an ongoing process that involves staff examining their own cultural background and upbringing, analyzing how their own 'cultural views' influence the way they see the world, and then striving to understand how their cultural view influences the way they understand our students and families."

Summary

Teacher leaders give back by identifying and championing the next generation of teacher leaders. If we are going to develop future teacher leaders, we must amplify the importance of teacher leadership in our communities and expose potential teacher leaders to opportunities. We must help all teachers feel that they have the potential to lead in their school community. There is a space for anyone who wants to lead.

Stop and Reflect

- ◆ Why is it important to discover potential teacher leaders?
- ◆ What is another way to locate potential teacher leaders?

16

How to Educate Teacher Leaders

> Managers tell people what to do; great leaders nurture people and help them realize they know what to do.

Education is inevitable in the teaching profession, and we must continue to learn and grow daily. When you locate potential teacher leaders, it is rewarding to guide them their journey to teacher leadership. Once you have connected with these teachers, your role is to nurture and enhance them by enabling them to flourish.

Why is it important to educate the leaders you discover? Well, they are probably going to make some mistakes in their career, but you may be able to save them from making a lot of mistakes. By doing so, you will make their journey a lot easier and encouraging for them. You will also boost their ability to make a positive impact in the world.

These new teachers need a safety net as they practice developing and discovering their leadership style. When I was a beginning teacher leader, this would have been helpful for me, especially when I felt I did not have a lot of room to make mistakes.

I remember hosting a community fair for my school when I was young in my career. I was looking for marketing tools to get students to attend. The school down the street was hosting an event one day—still a few days before my school's event. There were cars everywhere, and I asked my principal, Ms. Parks, if I could go put some fliers on cars. She told me, "Yes." However,

DOI: 10.4324/9781003229537-21

I neglected to tell her that the cars I was talking about were from a different school that was hosting an event in our same community.

Soon enough, the principal of the other school called and informed my principal about the fliers. She buzzed my room, and I was summoned to her office. Who expects the principal to call them during class time? I apologized for my rookie mistake. The moral of the story is this: educate and support new teacher leaders so they can avoid hang-ups large and small.

Every teacher is at a different stage in their career, and some may not need as much support as others. Make sure you assess where they are before deciding how to support and at what level to educate the teacher leader whom you are taking under your wing. You don't want to lose their interest or come off as demeaning, nor do you want to give them so little help that they feel lost.

From my experience, here are a few ways to educate teacher leaders in just the right way:

Create a New Teacher Leader Cohort

Teacher leaders lead cohorts in which they can learn from the potential teacher leaders and the potential teacher leader can learn from them. The cohort can be comprised of many potential teacher leaders and current teacher leaders. Or a potential teacher leader can be paired with a teacher leader. Ideally, cohorts with several teacher leaders and potential teacher leaders will meet monthly to discuss strategies and collaborate on various activities. A cohort will help support and nurture new teacher leaders.

Establishing groups of developing teacher leaders can help with educating and training them, as well as give them a group to bond with. Teacher leaders can mentor prospective teacher leaders by sharing knowledge in multiple ways (books, videos, discussions, etc.). Therefore, it is beneficial to find ways to share and learn from core group members. While in the groups, both mentors and mentees can share their experiences about what they've been learning or what challenges they face.

It's also important to keep a learning mentality. Teacher leaders are never finished learning, and they should point this out; mentees should not feel like they are the only ones learning. Relationships are based off of give and take. Everyone should be invested in the learning experiences.

Communicate Openly

It is important to create an open line of communication with prospective or new teacher leaders. You want them to trust you, so they can communicate with you openly. You can only support and guide them if they feel their voice matters. When talking to them, try to learn from them. Show that you care and be transparent about what you are learning and working toward.

My experience is that teachers are willing to give you input if you give them an opportunity to share; sometimes asking is all you need to do. Teacher leaders need encouragement on their path to teacher leadership, so establish a learning culture that is informative and enjoyable for them. You want to expand their learning. You don't know what you don't know, so it is important to create a safe space for them to share.

Provide Constructive Feedback

Feedback is essential to the success of teacher leaders of all ages, especially those who are starting out. It is important that they receive feedback on a continuous basis, and in positive ways, so they can feel valued and respected. To provide prospective teacher leaders with feedback, you can start by observing them teaching or leading an activity. You can read over the lesson plans that they have created. You can also provide feedback on any projects they are thinking about implementing.

As you work with the developing teacher leader, you will discover their strengths and weaknesses. Help them use them to turn their weaknesses into strengths by providing them with opportunities. When you provide feedback, you are creating healthy moments of learning and growing the potential teacher leaders.

Share Opportunities

Mature teacher leaders typically have many opportunities and know how to find more if they'd like to. New teachers typically do not. Teacher leaders should not just depend on the school leadership team, district, or state to provide all the opportunities that developing teacher leaders need. The difference can be made up by you, the teacher leader. You have established a rapport with organizations, and you can extend those opportunities by sharing them with those you mentor.

If you are recommending a teacher leader, you need to make sure that they are ready for the role. Don't throw them into something they aren't prepared for. You want to boost their confidence, not discourage them. They will appreciate the opportunities they are prepared for. But being prepared doesn't mean that the opportunities won't stretch them; you are helping them to learn from the organization while practicing their leadership skills, knowledge, and deposition.

One of the best types of opportunities you can share with developing teacher leaders are professional learning experiences. In addition to sharing experiences, you think will fit them, you can help them think through their own professional development opportunities that suit their needs. For these opportunities to be useful, they need to be opportunities that your mentee is interested in.

You can help a teacher leader to decide on the right action step for how to proceed in engaging in leadership by observing teacher leaders, attending professional development experiences, following the steps in this book, and so on. Finding opportunities for new teacher leaders to use their voices is especially helpful. Additionally, provide them with choices because, ultimately, they should have control over their own journey. Help them discover their interest, connect them with the opportunities they need, and give them space to grow.

Allow for Self-Educating

Speaking of giving teacher leaders space to grow, self-education was the best entry point for me on my journey to teach leadership. Throughout my book, you have heard me be a champion for the National Board process. Through self-discovery, I was able to navigate my path to teacher leadership.

In asking myself questions, reviewing the standards, and learning about the five core propositions of National Board, I had the chance to grow and establish my pathway. I had the chance to share the story of my students, families, community, and me. I had control of my learning experiences, and I was able to reflect and grow. That process literally ignited a spark with me to lead, collaborate, and impact student achievement. What sparks inspiration in the teacher leaders that you mentor may be different. There is no one-size-fits-all system. It doesn't matter what entry point they take, but you can help them find it.

Note: Here are some other suggestions on how potential teacher leaders can self-educate: books, blog post, conferences, professional development sessions, videos, articles, classroom observations, etc.

Summary

In developing teacher leaders, it is important to educate them about teacher leadership. There are things that they need to help them navigate through their leadership journey. While on their journey, they will need you to help support and encourage them. When you are working with them, it is important to focus on their needs and interests when suggesting learning experiences. They should have control over their destination; your role is to help them get there.

Stop and Reflect

♦ Why is it imperative for developing leaders to be engaged in worthwhile learning experiences?

♦ Why is it important to give developing teachers a voice in their learning experience?

♦ What would you add to the list of ways to educate developing teacher leaders? Why?

17

How to Reward Teacher Leaders

Your students and colleagues might forget some lessons but will never forget how you made them feel.

Teacher leaders are dedicated to their classroom, school, and community. They love what they do, and often they do it for little to no pay. They lead to make a difference in the students they teach and the school communities that they lead in. Teacher leaders can't raise salaries, but maybe we can begin to advocate in this area. Raising teachers' salaries may not be feasible, but there is another way to reward teacher leaders for what they do that is just as important (and sometimes more). That is to acknowledge their service, to praise them, and to help them feel valued and appreciated.

People will remember how you made them feel. Teacher leaders are no different. They will remember when you make them feel good about themselves. Good teacher leaders are irreplaceable, and they deserve to know that and to be acknowledged for the work that they do every day, all year round.

When I was inducted into the National Teacher Hall of Fame, my school hosted a Parade for a Champion drive through, hosted by my principal, Dr. Coleman. Community members, local news stations and newspapers, families, friends, and former and current students came out to support my accomplishment. I was grateful to receive recognition from my school community. It meant the world to me to see how people cared.

DOI: 10.4324/9781003229537-22

You know how great it feels to be rewarded for your sacrifices and hard work. As a teacher leader, it is your responsibility to give that feeling to other deserving teacher leaders. As you praise, you can influence your school's culture, and others will follow your lead.

The following are some ways you can reward the many people who deserve acknowledgment. In addition to teacher leaders, don't forget to give credit to your principal and district leaders and to community members.

Develop a System for Rewarding People

When establishing a reward system for teacher leaders, it is important to develop a clear and consistent plan. Teacher leaders can work alongside the administrative team to survey building-level teachers in developing a comprehensive plan. The plan should discuss the various moves and actions that a teacher leader should demonstrate to be selected as an exemplar teacher leader. The team can decide how frequent the teacher leader can be recognized. All teachers in the building should review the plan and adjust the criteria before adopting the reward system.

A rubric shows teachers how they and others will be scored, and it helps to eliminate bureaucracy. It can be used for promotions and non-monetary rewards such as awards and honors. When teachers are aware of how they will be rewarded and have some autonomy, it makes the process run smoothly. There will be no question of why someone is rewarded and others not.

The reward system should be personal, proportional, and timely. Teacher leaders need to understand that your success is their success. All teachers can appreciate how they will be acknowledged, and it can help with the climate and culture of the school.

Note: The school body should be aware (at least in part) of the reward system for teachers. Students can help to identify phenomenal teacher leaders as well. Sometimes, it is hard to see what all teachers are doing in the building, but students work with their teachers every day and know who influences them most.

Promote Community Care

It is important to promote community care in your community. The community can be a powerful support for teacher leaders. For instance, my superintendent and his leadership team dreamed big for teachers. Teachers received gift bags, a special dinner, students entertainment, and gift cards. The Supervisor of the Year received a $10,000 check and the District Teacher and Principal of the Year received cars. All of this was sponsored by community partners. When the community is involved, it can change the culture of how people view teacher leadership. You can get the community involved by inviting teacher leaders to speak at Parent Teacher Organizations meetings, and by informing parents about these teacher leaders' successes.

When you work together, everyone can see the importance of teacher leadership. You can invite community members into the teacher leaders' classrooms to showcase their work. Invite local businesses to provide discounts or gift cards to these teachers or invite them to share the teacher leaders' work on their marque or in their establishment. If there are parades, teacher leaders can participate in the parade for the community to see. Also, local sports teams can provide complementary tickets and recognition to show appreciation. Community members can send thank you notes. You can work with families and other leaders to locate community members to show that they care for teachers. When the community cares about the teachers, it changes the dynamic of how teachers and schools are viewed.

Spotlight Teacher Leaders' Stories

Teacher leaders help to recognize the development of other teacher leaders by nominating them for opportunities. When you see the great work that they are doing, you want to share their work with others. It is a great idea to find opportunities to shine a light on teacher leaders to create a channel for them. Showcasing the work and journey of other teacher leaders helps inspire them and scale their visions and their ideas while giving them credit for the hard work that they do. The main goal is to personally dedicate time and effort to amplify teacher leaders' stories.

Here are a few simple ways to spotlight deserving teachers:

♦ Post notes about them on the bulletin boards.
♦ Announce their accomplishments on the intercom.
♦ Decorate their doors.
♦ Have the students write and sing a song about the teacher leader.
♦ Set up an exhibit showcasing their work (but ask for their permission first).
♦ Put their favorite treat in their boxes or on their desks (but again, survey them first; they may not want sugary foods).
♦ Ask the principal if you can post a message celebrating them on the marquee. When I received my Ph.D., my first principal made an announcement on the intercom and placed my new status on the marquee
♦ Post their innovative ideas on the district and state websites (you may need to contact someone to do this).
♦ Treat them to lunch or dinner (provide a gift card).
♦ Invite a policymaker or the union leaders to their classrooms to highlight their work.
♦ Tell your local news station or newspaper about their work so they can acknowledge the teacher leader.
♦ Use social media outlets to show what they are doing.
♦ Provide them with a plaque or certificate for a job well done.
♦ Teacher of the Month Parking Spot.

Promote from Within

When you grow leaders, it is important to provide them with other opportunities to lead. Often, there are chances for teacher leaders to work with other teacher leaders. When those chances arise, you can provide the opportunities to the developing leader. In providing opportunities, you are allowing them to continue to evolve as a teacher leader. You will bring them joy and show them that you see the great work they are doing. You can work with other leadership team members in your building to create more opportunities for the new teacher leader. Listen to them, and you will discover what role they want to play.

Below are a few suggestions on how to promote from within. You will need the administration team to approve some of these suggestions, but teacher leaders can advocate for their peers to lead.

- ◆ Assign them a new teacher to mentor.
- ◆ Assign them a student teacher to mentor.
- ◆ Put them on a school or principal advisory board or instructional leadership team.
- ◆ Make their classrooms the model classroom, so people can learn from them.
- ◆ Support their innovative ideas—if they want to start a club or program, encourage it!
- ◆ Showcase their work on the school's website or at a faculty meeting.

Summary

Teacher leaders need to be rewarded, and one of the best forms of reward is praise. Lead out in praising other leaders in your school and community. Be new teacher leaders' best advocate by making sure that they receive praise, recognition, and honors. As they strive to climb up the ladder of success, it is vital that they are acknowledged for their efforts.

Stop and Reflect

- ◆ Why is it important to acknowledge teacher leaders?
- ◆ When was a time when your day was made through acknowledgment?
- ◆ How can your school and community be better about praising and rewarding their teacher leaders?

18

How to Lead by Example

Great leadership is more about what you do than about what you say.

Have you ever had someone inspire you in your career? Throughout my career, I have had several influential teacher leaders inspire me to do more for myself and my students. Some of those influential teacher leaders supported my career through mentorship. They allowed me to observe them in their classes, on social media, videos, or articles. These teacher leaders demonstrated high-quality instruction. Their example showed me the way.

Teacher leaders work with developing leaders primarily by demonstrating how they lead inside and outside the classroom. Teacher leaders demonstrate best practices, they don't just talk about them. They plant seeds of wisdom and inquiry in developing teacher leaders to help them to blossom into the leaders they can be. They demonstrate how to engage students in higher-order lessons, teach to mastery, collaborate with stakeholders, interpret and analyze data, and lead at various levels. They know that developing teacher leaders learn best when they see teacher leaders' model how they lead.

On the path to teacher leadership, teachers engage in gradual release with mentor teacher leaders. The process consists of the teacher leader modeling for them through observations; they collaborate collectively on projects; then the prospective teacher leaders take on their own project with limited support.

DOI: 10.4324/9781003229537-23

As a teacher leader, my goal is to build the capacity of other teacher leaders. I develop future leaders by allowing them to work alongside me to show them how to do it. It is my goal to help boost their confidence and skill levels where they are at the present time. It is important to make them feel comfortable, and it is my goal to ignite that spark in them that will give them the desire to lead. Here are a few suggestions on how to demonstrate the way forward with actions, not just words.

Set the Example in the Classroom

When modeling leadership, transparency is key: show them what leadership really looks like. You can invite future leaders into your classroom, so they can observe what you do to engage students. Teacher leaders show how they work their magic with their students. I cannot overestimate the value of developing leaders spending time in the classrooms of experienced teacher leaders. A great example of this, is mentoring student-teachers. This supports the teacher pipeline while creating future teacher leaders.

Developing teacher leaders are valuable to any school when they learn how to create worthwhile experiences for their students. What better way to learn than to see the best in action? Often, teachers go into their classrooms and close their doors and do not enter teacher leaders' room. This is a mistake. We must invite these teachers to stay after school to observe how other teacher leaders' plan for their classes and events, communicate with stakeholders, and multitask various projects.

Being a teacher leader is a balancing act, and it is important to allow newer leaders to see how to juggle everything. They need to analyze the teacher leaders' action and moves. They will then naturally pick up the actions and moves that are best for them. If they have questions, they can ask the teacher leaders. Also, this observation helps to establish a relationship with the teacher leaders and mentees. In building a relationship, the mentors and mentees continue to collaborate on projects, and work to develop their own initiatives.

Foster Collaboration

It is important that the teacher leaders feel supported by more experienced teacher leaders and building-level administrators. Once the teacher leaders have observed more experienced teacher leaders through multiple modeling and shadowing experiences, the mentee teacher leaders should have an opportunity to practice what they have learned and observed. An important part of that practice is collaboration with others.

These teachers can thrive when they have an outstanding team. Teacher leaders should collaborate on projects and planning with potential teacher leaders to boost their confidence and prepare them for greater responsibilities. Assigning roles helps all teacher leaders participate in the collaboration on equal footing. When experienced teacher leaders collaborate with newer teacher leaders, it helps to build their knowledge and strengthen their leadership skills for the benefit of students and the school communities. Overtime, the teacher leaders build trust, respect, and accountability with the potential teacher leaders.

Though important for training purposes, collaboration between teacher leaders should be ongoing, as teacher leaders understand how vital it is for the success of projects and initiatives, not to mention the education of students.

Empower Developing Teacher Leaders

My final suggestion is to empower potential teacher leaders to be leaders inside and outside their classrooms. Training is important, but ultimately, developing teacher leaders must be provided an opportunity to demonstrate what they have learned from their shadowing and collaboration experiences. The goal of building teacher leaders is to create space and opportunity to allow *them* to lead in their classrooms, buildings, districts, and communities.

Every teacher is different, so it is important to give them roles that they are ready to play in leadership. They may need some support, so it is important to discuss their plans and provide supportive feedback. The teacher leaders can ask careful questions to help develop newer teacher leaders to find clarity, meet expectations, and think critically about planning their lessons, projects, and activities.

Event-Planning Guide

When I first started leading events at my school, my assistant principal, Ms. Michelle Edwards-Watkins, would ask me probing questions to ensure that I was prepared. She also asked me what type of support that I needed. I appreciated that she attended the created events and that she praised me. I felt valued and appreciated as a beginning teacher leader.

Planning and creating events are great ways for developing teacher leaders to grow and find empowerment. The teacher leaders can help by providing a planning template or guide. Here is a guide that I created and find useful.

Answer the following questions.

◆ What are my goals or objectives for the event?
◆ Who do I need to communicate my ideas to?
◆ Who will attend the event?
◆ Parents?
◆ Students?
◆ Teachers?
◆ Community partners?
◆ Building level or district-level administrators?
◆ Will there be food?
◆ Who do I need on my team? What roles will the team members play?
◆ What is my marketing strategy?
◆ Flyers?
◆ Intercom announcements?
◆ Invitations (online or mail)?
◆ Posting on the website?
◆ Social media?

- ◆ Will there be activities or speakers?
- ◆ What do I need to put on an agenda?
- ◆ At what times will each item occur on the agenda?
- ◆ What documents will need to be submitted to the school?
- ◆ The agenda?
- ◆ A floor plan?
- ◆ Programs for the event?
- ◆ How will I set up for the event?

It is important to leverage your beginning teacher leaders to help shape the progress of programs and initiatives in your building. It is beneficial for these teacher leaders to contribute to school improvement as they explore new territory of teacher leadership.

Summary

A gradual release model supports potential teacher leaders to develop into effective teacher leaders. They should have the opportunity to observe teacher leaders in different settings through shadowing and modeling opportunities. Through observations, teacher leaders can learn the experienced teacher leaders' actions and strategies. Then the experienced teacher leaders collaborate with the newer teacher leaders to boost their confidence as they work together on projects or activities. When teacher leaders are empowered, they can be presented with leadership opportunities and given space to lead out on their own.

Stop and Reflect

- ◆ Why is it important to use a gradual release approach to support potential teacher leaders?
- ◆ How can you better empower new teachers?

Afterword

Encouragement and Advice: For the Love of Teacher Leadership

I love being a teacher leader. I have found it to be the most rewarding career ever! Each day, I have a chance to make a difference with my students, not only in my classroom but across the globe, because of the various opportunities and experiences that I have engaged in throughout my career. I am working with tireless commitment to all students, driven by my love for them and the profession.

I keep focused on addressing inequities among our marginalized students and love promoting racial harmony among my students. I believe in STEM, global learning, teacher leadership, and higher standards for all students. In my classroom, I can integrate all these subjects that I enjoy into my teaching.

I am so grateful for every opportunity from my principals, district leaders, and various organizations. I have made a difference in the lives of students, teachers, and the profession because of them. They believed in teacher leadership and provided me with an opportunity to lead. My classroom has truly become "My Happy Place!"

It has always been my goal to leave my footprints in the sand, so others may become inspired by my efforts. No good

DOI: 10.4324/9781003229537-24

deed is easy to accomplish, but it is rewarding when you can see the fruits of your labor.

Sergio says, "I love to see how students grow as students and as individuals. There is nothing in this world that can allow for greater joy than knowing you are making a positive difference in the lives of children."

Martha Mcleod says that she loves the classroom because of, "… the fire of passion I feel for sharing my love of science with students has not burned out yet. I truly enjoy seeing the excitement in a child's eyes when they behold a baby chick hatching; tasting a fresh carrot that they had planted and then harvested; or seeing a Baltimore Oriole for the first time through a spotting scope."

Michael Pope enjoys teaching children and preparing them for their futures. He believes, "… change begins with the young ones. In the future, they will be the ones making the hard decisions and shaping the world based on how they were inspired and instructed."

Teacher leaders give me hope for a better tomorrow. They are committed to their students. They love their students. And I cannot wait for you to become one of them.

Encouragement and Advice from Teacher Leaders

Here at the end of the book, I would like to leave you with a few words of encouragement from some of the teacher leaders you've met throughout this book and myself.

Wherever you are in your career, you must remember to savor the journey of teaching excellence, realizing that it is a vehicle to affect positive change in the lives of students. The journey is filled with challenges, achievement, and countless hugs to encourage you along the way and to remind you that the experiences are priceless!

Marjorie Brown believes, "Transcend yourself, listen, hear what the vocal people are saying, and try to find out what the voiceless feel. Analyze power relations—who is left out, what are people's agendas? Then analyze what you can do, and who you can draw on—everyone has something to contribute—remain open to all possibilities. Do not just act in a charitable way—try and make a long-term sustainable difference and empower students and people in the process. Create more equitable access to resources. Look at people holistically—from mental health, to skills, to interests."

Wendy Turner proclaims, "Future teacher leaders should know that we need you, you are valuable and most of all, kids need you and your passion, innovation, and your role modeling for others to be their best and pursue excellence relentlessly."

Wendy also says, "You've got to push past what is conventional and you've got to create kind of a contagious nature around what you believe in to help people understand the importance of what you're trying to do and how you're trying to positively impact students. And that's going to be unpopular with some people that have positional authority over you. So stay focused and grounded in what you are about, what you believe in, of course, being student centered and create those relationships that will help you get the work done and be brave. And if you feel like you're defeated sometimes or down and out or it's really difficult to continue being a teacher leader, take that time out, take that time for yourself, regroup and then go back to your core values and figure out how to pivot and move forward."

Sergio suggests, "Success is most readily achieved when all stakeholders are allowed to contribute and utilize their talents. As a leader, I see my role as a facilitator to support what others can bring to the table and achieve a shared goal. My advice to teacher leaders is to be that catalyst that will empower your community, and in turn, allow the most significant positive impact to ensue."

Michael Dunlea says, "Leadership looks different for different people and in different situations. Do not doubt your ability to lead or if you are already a leader because you are. Ask questions and take chances in leadership. We only make things better when we participate and not by spectating … Never underestimate the impact that teacher leadership will have on your career and on your students' learning. For me it was a life-ring that kept me afloat and, in the profession, and led to me being the best teacher I can be. Our students deserve nothing less."

Martha Mcleod provides the following advice. "The advice I would give teacher leaders is to honor and cherish the teachers whose top priorities involve what is best for students and not necessarily the highest test scores. All teachers have things they excel at, and student rapport should be a top priority when recruiting and evaluating a teacher."

Finally, Stephen Ritz says, "Behind every successful person there was a teacher, a mentor, an adult who believed in them; try to be that person for as many people as possible; kindness is contagious. This work requires courage, and the opposite of courage is not cowardice—it is conformity—because even a dead fish can go with the flow. So get out there and just keep swimming; there is a vast, beautiful, restless, and sometimes dangerous ocean waiting for you. You do not have to set yourself on fire to keep anybody else warm. … As a leader, I see my role as a facilitator to support what others can bring to the table and achieve a shared goal. My advice to teacher leaders is to be that catalyst that will empower your community, and in turn, allow the most significant positive impact to ensue."

As you continue your journey, I encourage you to do something different for yourself, community, and students. Remember, as Frederick Douglas said, "It is easier to build stronger children, than to repair broken men." The world needs you to impact the lives of students! They cannot do it without you!

For Product Safety Concerns and Information please contact our EU
representative GPSR@taylorandfrancis.com
Taylor & Francis Verlag GmbH, Kaufingerstraße 24, 80331 München, Germany

www.ingramcontent.com/pod-product-compliance
Ingram Content Group UK Ltd.
Pitfield, Milton Keynes, MK11 3LW, UK
UKHW021430080625
459435UK00011B/228

* 9 7 8 1 0 3 2 1 1 7 3 5 5 *